I HE♥RT RECRUITMENT

I HE♥RT RECRUITMENT

THE EIGHT STEPS TO LIMITLESS POSSIBILITY

FOR SORORITIES

COLLEEN COFFEY

AND

JESSICA GENDRON

A Product of Phired Up Productions, LLC

Created and published by

Phired Up Productions, LLC

230 Heritage Lane

Carmel, IN 46032

Authors: Colleen Elizabeth Coffey, Jessica Renee Gendron

Executive Editors & Foreword: Matthew Mattson, Joshua Orendi

I Heart Recruitment:

The Eight Steps to Limitless Possibility for Sororities

Coffey and Gendron

Printed in the United States of America

First Edition

http://www.PhiredUp.com

This book is dedicated to:

The Beta Pi and Delta Eta Chapters

It is the experiences that we have had and continue to have with each of you that drive our passion. You will always and forever be the most important women in our lives. We are honored to call the Alpha Sigma Tau sorority at Eastern Illinois University and Belmont University our homes.

With love to:

Kathy Beacker, Melissa Atkinson, and the 2004-2006 Fraternity Programs Staff and Friends – for all the pearls of wisdom.

Bob Dudolski: the most wonderful process challenger we know.

Our favorite Panhellenic Sisters and Fraternal Brothers

(you know who you are).

Especially our family and friends, who don't always understand what we do, but support us anyway.

Thanks to all of you for always encouraging us to GO FOR IT!

I Heart Recruitment is brought to you by Phired Up Productions, LLC – the company that gave the college fraternity world **Good Guys:** *The Eight Steps to Limitless Possibility for Fraternity Recruitment* by: Matthew Mattson and Joshua Orendi

Special thanks to the Women's Curriculum Development Committee of Phired Up Productions, LLC

Committee Members:

Beth Conder, Alpha Chi Omega
Ashley Dye, Pi Beta Phi
Jessica Gendron, Alpha Sigma Tau
Renee Rambeau, Chi Omega
Kristin Torrey, Delta Gamma
Colleen Coffey, Alpha Sigma Tau, Chair

The authors also wish to thank the following people for their help in the editing process:

Amanda Bureau	Lori Hart Ebert
Dan Bureau	Danielle Kuglin
Patricia Carey Floren	Jennifer Pope

PHIRED UP PRODUCTIONS is an education firm

providing recruitment services to membership organizations. We offer an integrated menu of services ranging from recruitment training and values education to action planning for organizations, institutions, and individuals – all based on our core philosophy, "The Eight Steps to Limitless Possibility."

Phired Up Productions has delivered training and programming to the college fraternity/sorority community since 2002. With the publication of **Good Guys** in 2006, the company became widely recognized as *The Recruitment Experts*.

Our message is especially for customers that desire a higher quantity of higher quality individuals involved in their organization – and who are interested in long-term, limitless success. We specialize in helping college student organizations including fraternities and sororities; service groups, cultural and religious organizations, admissions, housing and orientation groups; and other student associations. Outside of our main collegiate market, we partner with community organizations including business and commerce groups; charities and not-for-profit organizations; gender and cultural issue groups; fraternal organizations; businesses; and religious institutions.

www.PhiredUp.com

TABLE OF CONTENTS

GO FOR IT, GIRL!

Throughout *I Heart Recruitment* you will find practical applications to improve your recruitment results immediately. Pay special attention to the sections entitled **"Go For It, Girl!"** These sections provide exercises and activities to help you get immediate results.

FOREWORD

BY

MATTHEW MATTSON & JOSHUA ORENDI
AUTHORS OF **GOOD GUYS** AND
FOUNDERS OF PHIRED UP PRODUCTIONS

*Once upon a time, there were these two guys (Matt and Josh) who wrote a book and thought they were smart. They had talked with fraternity men about Dynamic Recruitment techniques for many years and, one day, they decided to try to talk with sorority women about the same topic. So, there they were, feeling like very smart authors indeed (perhaps, even experts). The women listened, laughed, and took notes. They said, "This information is really good. My sisters need to hear this message. BUT ... **women's recruitment is different than men's recruitment**."*

For a few brief moments, we thought we could learn enough about sorority recruitment to tweak the message, offering a "new" version of the book and program. (That was a dumb idea.) We knew the concepts that we'd used for fraternity men would work in the sorority world, but we also knew that women deserved a book of their own – a message of their own – one written for women, by women. It was clear that we needed help.

Colleen Coffey and Jessica Gendron were the right women to take a message that began in a masculine world, tear it up, toss it around, and put their feminine touch on it. They produced a world-class book, a book that is far superior to the original work, in our humble opinions. Colleen's visionary ability and real-life experience, which includes academic research on driving sorority recruitment results, paired with Jessica's unique brand of practical, experience-based insight and sense of humor were the perfect ingredients to help sorority women understand what *limitless possibilities* are really all about. And, so, the idea for *I Heart Recruitment* was born.

As you read further along in this book, you'll come to a lesson about mules and horses (Step 3). We used this concept (gathering up the "doers" to get things done) as a practical application exercise while writing this book. Colleen, Jessica, and the two of us gathered up some of the true work horses in the sorority industry to serve on a committee that would help us produce an amazing book. The women (as listed at the front of this book) who helped with this project are amazing examples of how great results naturally come from great people doing what they do best. And, to say the least, we're very grateful for their hard work.

While reading *I Heart Recruitment,* it will be easy to see the great ideas throughout the book as little hints and tips here and there. But, take a moment to step back and take a look at the message in the book from a wider perspective. This book is a blueprint for a revolution. It is an outline of an uprising. It is the plan for a rebellion against mediocrity. Recruitment is at the core of all sorority issues, both good and bad. Recruitment is also at the core of what we see as the beginning of a revolution in the Greek world.

Are you a revolutionary? Are you brave enough to challenge the status quo? Are you courageous enough to stand up against the mediocrity of the present in favor of the greatness of the future? It all begins with choosing to recruit differently. Colleen and Jessica will explain why and how, but, for now, just understand that the revolution begins with you. And it begins now.

NOBODY TEACHES THIS STUFF

Hi! We're Colleen and Jessica, the authors of *I Heart Recruitment*. We are both sorority women who are passionate about sorority recruitment, but don't be fooled, it hasn't always been that way. So, before we begin, we are going to tell you a little bit about ourselves and where our own recruitment story started.

Colleen began her sorority life when she was initiated into Alpha Sigma Tau sorority at Belmont University in Nashville, TN. Jessica, also a member of Alpha Sigma Tau, did her undergraduate work at Eastern Illinois University in Charleston, IL. Our experiences, though very different, were both quite fantastic.

We met each other while both working professionally as Traveling Educational Consultants for ΑΣΤ. We spent most of our time working with chapters on, of all things, recruitment issues. The truth is that we succeeded in a lot of areas as consultants. Overall, we thought we were pretty good at recruiting new members. But, boy oh boy, did we have another thing coming. Looking back on our consultant days, we realized that we were actually pretty pushy and primarily focused on "helping" each chapter get enough "numbers" to fill quota or be at total. Our focus was on the *quantity* of members because, in our minds, size equaled success.

To some degree that might be true, but when it came to recruitment, we were looking at it in completely the wrong way. Instead of focusing on quality people, organizational purpose, sorority values, and interpersonal skills, we became really good at convincing women that sorority membership was for them. We helped chapters recruit some amazing women during that year, so it wasn't all for nothing. However, if we knew then what we know now about recruitment and, quite frankly, life, we may have done things a little bit differently.

To be completely honest, Colleen didn't really think her chapter struggled with recruitment when she was in college. Each fall, her chapter would go through formal recruitment, make quota, and call it a day. Each spring they would have one to three continuous open recruitment events, recruit a few more new members, and that was it. Recruitment talk only came around twice a year. As you will learn in this book, recruitment is not a twice-a-year type of activity. Whether you can ask women to join all year long or are limited by policies that require you to ask them on one specific day a year, recruitment is a year-round process. Don't worry, we promise to explain all the details later!

Jessica's experience was a bit different. Eastern Illinois University has a much larger Greek Community than Belmont. While Jessica came from a big chapter, it never seemed that they were quite big enough. Each year they would almost make quota and almost fill total; however, instead of spending the time after formal recruitment celebrating their newest members, the pressure was on to keep recruiting. At Eastern Illinois, making quota and being at total equaled success. It also separated, in the campus mindset, the good sororities from the bad. Again, this is yet another common misconception when it comes to sorority recruitment. You will learn later in the book that *quantity* or *quality* alone do not necessarily equal success.

Maybe you can relate to one of these experiences and maybe you can't. Either way, we know we can relate with your story. We have traveled across the country for several years, working in many different capacities (National Sorority Officers, Campus Administrators, Graduate Advisors, and professional speakers) on every type of campus and in every type of environment. Girl, do we have stories for you! This book is a culmination of our experiences and the experiences of others, not to mention mere trial and error. Whatever type of chapter you come from, whatever type of campus, and no matter how big or small your membership numbers are, you will get something out of this book – we promise.

Unfortunately, no one ever actually *taught* us the "right" way to recruit. We have learned how to recruit the hard way, through years of advising struggling chapters. We have watched how the self-esteem of the groups we work with is constantly threatened by the fact that they are not the biggest (a.k.a. the best, whatever that means) chapters on campus. We have observed many groups recruit the "cutest girls," completely disregarding how those women fit in to their organization's mission and values or what they will contribute to their chapter. We have observed a consistent theme with sororities, in that the majority of the recruitment efforts are focused on one time large events and membership selection processes are based solely on how well a potential new member can sell herself in 30 minutes or less. We have also come to find out that these methods (and many others) are not producing the best results, thus causing chapters to be met with a lack of retention, motivation, and confidence.

This is why we want to share our message with you. This book is based on the premise that if you had a system to recruit a higher *quantity* of higher *quality* members, you would have more money as a chapter, more friends as a chapter, more energy as a chapter, and you could do more fun things as a chapter. Essentially, a better amount of better people makes a better organization or, more precisely, a better amount of people to *choose* from makes a better organization. Plus, it doesn't have to take a painful amount of work to achieve success!

We also believe strongly in the power of Panhellenic sisterhood. Through years of experience we have learned that we, as sorority women, are all in this together. So, be sure to share our message with *all* sorority sisters (yes, we mean other sororities and other chapters of your organization), not just *your* sorority sisters.

We are proud to share with you what we so desperately needed throughout our own sorority careers. We wrote this book because we believe that success in recruitment is often directly related to the self-esteem of the chapter's members and we want to teach you the things we never knew.

SO, WHAT'S WITH THE TITLE?

Recruitment.

What do you think of when you hear that word? Our guess is that, for most of you, it makes you cringe just a little bit. Maybe this word makes you think of late night skit practices and membership selection processes that go into the wee hours of the morning. Maybe it makes you think about the sense of urgency you sometimes feel to recruit more women so you can be a bigger chapter and people will stop bothering you. Maybe the whole thing confuses you. Or maybe you remember your heart breaking when your chapter neglected to select that one special potential new member that you just *knew* was going to join your chapter and become your little sister. Maybe a complicated recruitment process even affected you Whatever the case, we want this book to change your mind and your HE♥RT.

Recruitment should be enjoyable; it shouldn't cause anxiety. It should be a time of celebration, not of heart-break. When done right, recruitment is actually pretty easy and doesn't require you to lose sleep, miss class, act fake, or give up your life to make it work.

I Heart Recruitment is much more than just a title; it is a state of mind. Do you HEART, and we really mean LOVE, recruitment? If you read this book, take it all in, and put these lessons into practice, we believe that you will.

DISCLAIMER

Before we begin, there are a few things you should know:

♥ We're not going to lie. This book is not 100% applicable for 100% of sororities or Panhellenic communities. It is, however, written so that all sorority chapters and Panhellenic communities can use some, if not all, of this book to create a more values-based, results-driven chapter or Panhellenic community.

♥ We are not the National Panhellenic Conference (NPC) nor do we represent the NPC. This is not the NPC Manual of Information nor does it refer to Unanimous Agreements. We are merely two women offering a system of recruitment best practices for sororities. We did take into consideration the vast variance of recruitment structures across the country as well as from institution to institution. However, we might not have specifically considered *your* individual Panhellenic community's recruitment regulations, contact rules, or other local Panhellenic bylaws. Before you put any of these *Dynamic Recruitment* strategies into practice, please consult your Panhellenic Council, Greek Advisor, Chapter Advisor, or your NPC delegate to verify you are compliant with all applicable policies. Since you are reading this book, we know that you're smart women and *you* have the power to influence the policies that govern you. Don't be afraid to ask questions about the rules, regulations, and policies that influence your recruitment potential – especially if they seem to get in the way of your recruitment success.

♥ We believe in the power of a year-round recruitment process. We also believe in the value of a properly run formal recruitment process. Formal recruitment is only a PART of a year-round *Dynamic Recruitment* system.

♥ Additionally, our idea of *Dynamic Recruitment* does not include funnier skits, better desserts, cooler themes, or matching outfits. If that is what you were hoping to get from this book, close the book, put it back in the bag, and return it to the store. NO, WAIT! We are just kidding! You need this book the most, so please read on.

♥ Finally, you should know that we consulted some of the best sorority women in the field while writing this book. We have provided you with a framework to create a more dynamic recruitment process, a more dynamic chapter, and a more dynamic sorority community. This book will educate you on how to be better, more intentional, and more focused when it comes to getting the recruitment results you dream of. We did this all with a little humor. It's okay, we can laugh at ourselves, it's kind of funny.

THE 8 STEPS TO LIMITLESS POSSIBILITY

Get excited, ladies, because now it's time to get down to business.

We share a bond. You understand, just like we do, that our lifelong commitment to sorority values is rooted in the virtue of humanity. All that is good in the world is represented in sorority women – most of the time, anyway. You also understand, like we do, that sometimes it can be downright hard to convince others of your sorority's value and get them to join you in a lifelong friendship.

Every woman in your organization has sworn to uphold the same oath, pledging a life-long commitment to your founding principles and the perpetuation of your sisterhood. The actualization of that commitment to living and growing the organization determines your success as a sorority. In practice, that means growing the *quantity* and *quality* of your membership. It also means realizing the power of Panhellenic sisterhood and a strong Greek community. Have you ever heard someone say, "You are only as strong as your weakest link?" Well, it's true! The stronger all sororities are on your campus; the better your community is as a whole.

Bottom line – one of the first things you promised to do when you went through your ritual was to RECRUIT (so, get busy if you aren't already doing so), because if your Greek community is not the best it can be, you will not be the best you can be (so, take off your cool cap and make some new friends).

The systematic approach presented in this book is a program for maximizing your potential as a world-class sorority chapter and, moreover, for becoming a member of a truly outstanding Panhellenic community. The Eight Steps to Limitless Possibility is often thought of as just a recruitment model, but if you look closely, you'll see that it is much more than that. It is a system to build a healthy, self-sustaining, values-based organization that achieves unimaginable success.

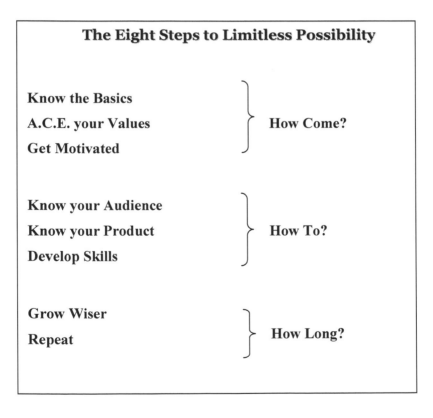

The Eight Steps to Limitless Possibility

Know the Basics
A.C.E. your Values
Get Motivated } How Come?

Know your Audience
Know your Product
Develop Skills } How To?

Grow Wiser
Repeat } How Long?

Introduction to The Eight Steps to Limitless Possibility

We provide detailed descriptions and instructions for each of these eight steps throughout the book. But, for now, here is a brief description of how The Eight Steps can work together.

Steps 1, 2, and 3 are the "How Come?" Steps. These three steps help answer the question, "How come?" or "Why is recruitment important?" Effective chapters always begin by understanding their purpose and developing their own motivation to achieve desired outcomes. They systematically maximize their chapter's total membership based on their founding purpose and shared values. Once the foundation is set (Step 1), members have agreed to achieve, communicate, and expect congruent values-based behavior (Step 2), and they have a unifying dream providing motivational fuel (Step 3), they can then begin to take actions to grow the *quantity* and *quality* of their chapter sisters and Greek community members.

Next we learn how to answer the "How To?" question with Steps 4, 5, and 6. These steps help to develop an understanding of your target audience (Step 4), a deeper knowledge of the value your organization provides (Step 5), and the interpersonal skills necessary to confidently communicate your organization's values and value to the public (Step 6). Overall, the "How To?" Steps give your chapter or community the necessary tools to succeed in recruitment.

Finally, Steps 7 and 8, the "How Long?" Steps, remind you that long-term sustained growth and success requires constantly seeking wisdom from external and internal sources (Step 7). Furthermore, long term success is supported by the implementation of repeatable systems and training that instill positive patterns of behavior in all of your members (Step 8). The "How Long?" steps provide you with a glimpse on how to proceed, how to build a repeatable system for success, and where to go next.

This eight step system guides you in a sequential learning experience that develops patterns of behavior – habits – for you and your members. As soon as you are familiar with this program, we insist that you do two things:

1. Practice the principles by putting your plan into action. **Go for it, girl!**

2. Share the program with someone else as it was taught to you. **Preach on, sister!**

"The secret of getting ahead is getting started."

~ Sally Berger~

GOOD GIRLS

After hours of heated debate, the chapter finally decides on T-shirt designs, party themes, decorations, outfits, chants for recruitment, and, of course, who is going to be in the skit. The chapter has spent an entire semester preparing for recruitment. Once recruitment draws near, the chapter spends countless hours blowing up balloons, making banners, decorating the chapter room, practicing their skit, and checking outfits to prepare for the big week.

The chapter also invests most of its available funds and hundreds of hours into preparing for the arrival of the potential members. The All-Panhellenic events are okay, but the real recruiting happens at the chapter's own well-rehearsed recruitment parties. The chapter is known particularly for their skit party and has a lot of pride in that specific event.

No one is quite sure who will attend the skit party, but everyone is sure it will be a HUGE success. Potential members will be practically asking for bids by the dozens when they see the skit and how well the chapter can make their recruitment efforts come together. Special care has been given to cleaning and decorating the house, and selecting the perfect food and drink. The chapter is now prepared for the best recruitment ever.

The party goes relatively well since everyone had a good time. The potential new members laughed at the skit, (but not nearly as much as the members did), hardly any potential members ate the food or commented on the decorations, and some of the chapter's favorite potential members weren't there. Additionally, no one could really remember more than a handful of the potential members by name or what they looked like, because everyone spent the majority of the time watching the skit – not talking or interacting.

As recruitment comes to a close, the sisters gather in a room together to begin the infamous voting process. A few women slide through with a unanimous "yes." Then, a sister in the back of the room questions a potential member's reputation and another sister yells out, "Yeah, I don't even know this girl." Another says, "Isn't that the frumpy girl in the pink?" Yet another pipes up, "She's so cute, you guys!" Finally, a respected sister calmly says, "Trust me; she will be an asset to the chapter." A few others chime in, "I think we should give her a chance. She was cute, outgoing, and she already knows tons of fraternity guys." With that, the criteria has been set and the chapter is now several hours deep in a hot room to determine who is "cute" enough, or who will be enough of an "asset to the chapter" to receive a bid.

The chapter fills quota, but only half of the bids are from their first bid list. The chapter is shocked and disappointed! However, the sisters relieve some heartache by reminding themselves that – just like last semester – they still managed to get "some really good girls."

Did anything sound familiar in that story?

If you can relate even a little, we're laughing right along with you. It's okay. You're involved with a chapter stuck in a traditional recruitment process that we call *Static Recruitment*.

If you can't completely relate to that story, good for you! You are probably either involved in a new chapter or you are fortunate enough to be a part of a small population of sororities today that practice *Dynamic Recruitment*. *Dynamic Recruitment* is the year round process of proactively seeking high quality women through a successful system built upon daily patterns of behavior that produce results.

It is important to note that some of you may be involved in a chapter like Colleen's. Remember, her group would make quota and total through formal recruitment and call it a day. Those types of chapters often do well because of popularity and if that describes your chapter, congratulations. However, that does not mean that your current recruitment practices do not need some improvement. Perhaps your chapter is like Colleen's, yet still has trouble with retention, maybe you feel as if you do not know your new members well, or maybe you could benefit from shifting your focus just a little bit.

This book is for you whether or not that story was exactly like your reality. *I Heart Recruitment* is a book meant to take your chapter and your community from good to great, from *static* to *dynamic*, or even from *dynamic* to **unbelievable**.

We've learned from our experiences working with various sororities at all types of schools – big, small, private, public, urban, rural, etc. – that there are a few commonalities that might have resonated for you in that story.

1. Sororities have some traditions that could be changed. A lot of sororities keep doing the same old things and keep getting the same old results.

2. Many sororities have a crippling illness: *Dependecitis.* Dependecitis (the primary symptom being an unhealthy dependence on formal recruitment) is a nasty disease that makes all chapters infected believe they have to spend a lot of money and time on planning their formal recruitment events in order to recruit members.

3. No matter how incredible your formal recruitment events are, how funny your skit is, how cute your T-shirts are, or what kind of food you serve, not many women go through recruitment and join because of those things.

4. The fact is that only a small percentage of the women on your campus sign up and participate in formal recruitment. These women are what we call "Always Joiners" and they probably make up about 15% of your potential recruitment pool. Your recruitment efforts should be focusing on the 70% of women that are the "Maybe joiners." These "Maybe joiners" don't sign up to watch you put on skits and decorate your house for a week; to

them, formal recruitment is a bizarre ritual and more than a little intimidating (we'll explain more later).

5. The sad truth about recruitment is that the chapters on campus who recruit the most STRANGERS are often considered the *winners*. This is the epitome of *Static Recruitment*.

The story about a typical *Static Recruitment* period may not apply to you and your chapter 100%. It may not even totally apply to your campus if your Panhellenic Community uses partially, minimally, or non-structured recruitment. However, we have a feeling that most readers will be able to find something oddly familiar in that story. Your chapter probably falls somewhere on a continuum of the difference between a sorority that is dependent on *Static Recruitment* and a sorority that is committed to the ideas in this book, practicing *Dynamic Recruitment*.

Whether you realize it or not, your current recruitment process is good. Why? Well, simply put, *it was good enough to get you*. We can't help but be excited that you've decided to make it great.

Every reader of this book has different needs. Some are desperate for recruitment help because their chapter's or Greek community's immediate survival depends on it. If that's you, we suggest you take the contents of this book pretty seriously. Other readers might be happy with their current recruitment system. If that's you, we recommend that you look for a couple of ideas in this book that might help you become even better.

An important lesson to start with is: **You can't recruit who you don't know.** If this is true (and it obviously is), then you know that before you can recruit someone you have to meet them, and if only a small percentage of women are signing up for formal recruitment, then you never have a chance to recruit a lot of really great women (the ones that don't sign up or show up for formal recruitment).

Further, no one should regulate your ability to build relationships or have friendly contact with potential new members outside of your formal (or even partially-structured) recruitment period. Joining a sorority is a life-long commitment similar to marriage, so it is important to get to know the women you are recruiting. Before most couples get married, they spend at least a little time dating. After they date for a while, there may come a proposal for marriage. After the proposal, more time is spent being engaged. Then, and only then, is there a wedding (and the lifetime commitment). Recruitment on most campuses is like going on three 20 minute speed dates in a week with some random person and then saying to him or her, "I guess you seem pretty normal. I can work on making you perfect after the wedding. Wanna get married tomorrow?" Would you really marry someone that you had only known for a week?

We didn't think so...

Membership in a sorority can be the most valuable experience on any college campus today for women. There is no other opportunity for a young woman that offers the breadth and depth of real-life learning and leadership opportunities than the sorority experience does. We believe in the idea of sorority and we believe that a revolution can begin right now – with you – to take the college sorority movement into the world of limitless possibilities. Recruitment is truly the lifeblood of a sorority. Without it, the organization doesn't exist. The revolution begins now and it starts with better recruitment practices that bring a consistently higher *quantity* of higher *quality* women into the greater Panhellenic community.

GO FOR IT, GIRL!

Experience the limitless possibilities that await your chapter right away by applying the following ideas:

♥ Share the *Static Recruitment* story with your sisters and see which parts they identify with. Use this to lead the conversation about implementing the changes suggested in this book.

♥ Ask the most involved leaders in your chapter about the moment they knew they were going to join and the person who most influenced their decision. This insight provides wisdom into more effective ways to attract top talent.

♥ Think about the women who never really got involved the way you hoped or who quit the organization early on. Why did they join? Who influenced their decision? And what lessons can you learn from their early departures to improve your recruitment and retention efforts?

♥ Ask yourself and your fellow chapter sisters which recruitment efforts actually get results. What actually works to get amazing and committed women into your organization? What things do you do to get new women to join your chapter which might look ridiculous to an outsider? We are confident that you did not join your sorority because of their cool balloons, free food, or a killer chant. FYI: All that stuff seems pretty silly to potential new members and especially weird to other students.

HOW COME?

The "How Come?" Steps (1, 2, and 3) are about understanding who you are as a chapter holistically, as well as who you are as an individual chapter member. They are also about an understanding of what type of potential new members you are seeking. We ask you to think critically about what you value as a person, organization, and community. This section should help you examine how you are spending your time, why you recruit, and what is most important about sorority life.

"If you have knowledge, let others light their candles in it."

~ Margaret Fuller~

STEP ONE: KNOW THE BASICS

Let's start at the very beginning: Why is knowing the basics of anything important? Well, let's take botany for example. Most of you are thinking, "Botany? What are they talking about?" Okay, we don't really mean "botany," we really mean "plants." Plants have two very basic needs: water and sunlight. Without those two things, plants can't exist. Sure, there are other things like good soil, fertilizer, a bigger pot, and pruning that will help a plant to be successful, but a plant MUST have water and sunlight to survive. If you don't know the basics of plants, it is very likely that your plants will fail to be successful (a.k.a. they will, sadly, die). As a sorority or sorority community, it is important that you "Know the Basics" and work on those, or your organization or community will fail to be successful. We do not want your metaphorical "plant" (your community/chapter) to wilt or, even worse, die; so listen up!

If botany doesn't get your heart pumping with recruitment love, then let's try a different approach – sports. For those of you who are big sports fans, you're probably thinking, "Yes! This book isn't all *girly* talk after all!" However, for those of you who would rather sit through a two hour chapter meeting than watch a two hour baseball game, we are about to teach you something about baseball, so get excited, you just might learn something. Regardless of how you feel about sports, this example is a pretty cool way to think about the "basics."

Major League Baseball is a complex business, but one thing you hear "expert" analysts talking about all the time is the fact that the best baseball teams are built on "pitching and defense." That's quite a statement considering no runs are scored by either pitchers or fielders while they're on defense (runs are scored when the team is on offense). Yet, you hear time after time that the experts believe "pitching and defense" to be the fundamentals of a great baseball team.

The suggestion is then, that when a General Manager builds a baseball team, he should first focus on getting great pitching and great defense – then and only then, should he consider anything else. Home run hitters, base stealers, new stadiums, fancy uniforms, and the flavor of cotton candy sold by the vendors are all secondary details when compared to "pitching and defense." A great baseball team knows the basic components that are necessary to win a championship and they focus on making those basic components, the fundamentals, truly remarkable.

Even if you're not a baseball fan, you can probably think of times in your life in which it is important to first focus on the fundamentals – to Know the Basics. So, in our sorority context, before we can discuss the details of how to build a healthy organization through effective recruitment strategies, we first must understand the very basic fundamentals of sororities – our organizations' core composition.

The first step in The Eight Steps to Limitless Possibility, "Know the Basics," asks you to consider your very make up as an organization. What are the basic ingredients? What makes it tick?

What basic needs do you have as a chapter? What has kept you around this long?

The answers to these questions are simpler than you might think. There are two basic needs that make your sorority work. Those two basic things are at the genesis of your organization and that have kept your sorority around for decades: ***People and Purpose.*** Your chapter, just like your organization's founding chapter, needs a bunch of women and a reason to get together. If your chapter only had one of these, what would it be?

- A group of women without a purpose is simply a crowd of ladies.
- A purpose without people to fulfill it is just a fluffy idea floating around in space.

Put these two things together though – People and Purpose – and what do you get?

You get a membership organization equipped to change the lives of its members and everyone around them. The Girl Scouts, church groups, U.S. Military, and especially sororities are all examples of membership organizations rooted in the basics of People and Purpose. You get an organization just like your sorority. What makes every organization special are its specific purpose and the unique individuals who come together, committed to that purpose. But, "Knowing the Basics" is only the first part of this step. You also have to focus on the basics.

The process of knowing the basics looks something like this: Recruit members, they develop together through the purpose of the organization, those new members recruit more members; and then they develop together through the purpose of the organization. It is an endless cycle, as long as it isn't ignored, and it is your very lifeblood as a sorority. This is the way that an organization is made and sustained.

It only makes sense, then, that this basic, natural set of needs created by the cycle of membership should be concentrated upon and fulfilled before other needs of the organization's own hierarchy. If you focus on recruitment and individual character development more than you focus on what's going to be on next semester's recruitment T-shirts and who is taking whom to the next social event, you'll start seeing significant positive change. The basics of sorority – People and Purpose – are like the basics of plants and baseball: straightforward and finite.

This is pretty simple stuff, we know, but ask yourself the following question: What percentage of time at your last chapter meeting was spent talking specifically about a real plan to get more members and/or how best to develop the character of your current membership so that you would have a higher quality organization? Our experience has shown us that almost all failed sorority chapters can trace their failure back to a lack of focus on People and Purpose.

The Pareto Principle, a brilliantly simple truism from an incredible economist, states that 80% of the results of any organization usually come from 20% of the effort. Your challenge is: can you flip that upside down?

If you spent 80% of your chapter's energy on the areas of your needs that currently receive about 20% (People and Purpose), wouldn't your chapter's *quantity* of *quality* members increase dramatically? And, if that happened, wouldn't many of the major headaches you have as a chapter leader disappear because you'd have more women, better women (those who fulfill their commitments, pay their dues, and don't embarrass you), more money, and more time? Sounds good so far, right?

On your campus or within your inter/national sorority, you can probably think of a chapter that existed just a few years ago, but is no longer an organization. Why did they disband, get shut down, or fizzle away? It almost always comes back to People and/or Purpose: Either a failure to recruit good members or the group ends up drifting away from the values established by the sorority or fraternity's founders. A strong organization must be deeply rooted in these fundamentals. Step 1, "Know the Basics," is simple, but important nonetheless. We often take for granted the very things that give our sorority life and help it thrive. Shift your focus. Get more *people* to achieve the sorority's *purpose.* Do what matters first.

GO FOR IT, GIRL!

Experience the limitless possibilities that await your chapter right away by applying the ideas provided here:

♥ Evaluate your chapter calendar. What portion of your chapter events focus on People and Purpose? Empower your chapter's secretary to maintain a journal keeping track of time and resources to make sure that the focus is on the basics.

♥ Evaluate your next chapter meeting. What percentage of time is spent specifically on the fulfillment of the chapter's purpose and results-producing recruitment activities? Are you as focused as you should be on these basic things?

♥ Evaluate your chapter's budget. What percentage of money is spent on things that actually grow the chapter's membership in *quantity* and *quality*? How much money is used on less important things? We aren't just talking about the recruitment budget, but things that actually get women to join. How much money are you investing in developing People and Purpose?

♥ Evaluate your recruitment efforts during the 10 weeks *after* formal recruitment. Are you meeting just as many potential new members? Are you putting the same amount of effort into developing relationships with potential members? Are you extending invitations for membership all semester long? Remember, you can't recruit who you don't know.

"For what is done or learned by one class of women becomes, by virtue of their common womanhood, the property of all women."

~ Elizabeth Blackwell~

STEP TWO: A.C.E. YOUR VALUES

Step 2 is about the *quality* of your current and future members. It is also about whether or not your chapter abides by the "truth in advertising" law.   In this step, your organization re-commits itself to Achieving, Communicating, and Expecting (A.C.E.) the values of the sorority.

Doing what you say you'll do as an organization is vital for successful recruitment. In order to build your foundation, you must actively exemplify the very values that you espouse. Those values are displayed internally through your rituals, teachings, and code of conduct Externally, those values are announced loudly through your publications, history, mission statement, the daily actions of your members, and, yes, even your t-shirts. People outside of your organization have a predetermined idea of what you are supposed to represent, so you are expected to do what you say you will do. We have confidence in you and we know you are probably pretty smart about all this stuff. So, go for it, girl – A.C.E. those values! Don't worry, we'll give you a little bit of help with the following explanation:

- **Achieving:** To achieve your values, you must first know and embrace them. Once you have pried open the secret closet, blown the dust off the ritual book, and taken a peek inside, take the time to consider what changes in your organization and personal life need to be made in order to ACHIEVE what your founders hoped for. If you aren't working to achieve your sorority's values, you may be leading your potential members into something they aren't expecting and that your founders did not intend.

- **Communicating**: Your words and your actions in public are clearly COMMUNICATING your beliefs. Every minute of every day your members are sending messages to the world about what a sorority woman that wears your letters is all about. People interpret the actions of your members as a statement of your organizational values. This is great, if the message is on target with your stated purpose. So, what exactly is your chapter communicating?

- **Expecting**: You must also EXPECT the values of the organization to be upheld by your members, potential members, and especially by yourself. This means holding each other accountable to the oath that you make as sisters to your sorority. Potential new members (and, quite frankly, the rest of the world) can tell when a chapter lacks integrity. Do you actually hold your members accountable to the things you say are expected of them?

In recruitment, when you A.C.E. Your Values, you:

- Create a better public image.

- Get more sisters involved in recruitment.

- Prepare your sisters to help others understand your organization (because you understand it).

- Establish a benchmark for identifying quality potential new members.

When you A.C.E. Your Values, you make your actions congruent with the values of your organization and your community. A.C.E.-ing our values is not exemplified by catty, gossipy, shady, or shallow recruitment practices. The purpose of recruitment and the values of your organization are negated when your members purposefully break the rules, sabotage another chapter, or talk bad about other sororities during recruitment time (or any time, for that matter). As a sorority woman in your community, your responsibility is to provide a positive public image of Greek life by portraying every organization in a positive manner, whether or not they are your own, and encouraging people to join your COMMUNITY (there is a place for everyone who wants to be a part). That is how you can A.C.E. your values.

Share Your Ritual with Non-Members

The thought of sharing your esoteric ritual with non-members probably freaks you out a little bit. We know. It's OK and we'll explain. At one time, early on, being a secret society was a necessary part of most sororities' survival. Unfortunately, today, uncertainty about which parts of the sorority are to be kept private, coupled with a fear of being the one girl to let out ancient secrets, has created a hush so powerful that most sorority women rarely tell potential members anything at all about their organization's values. Worse yet, sorority women got so good at keeping secrets that many of our own sisters can't even communicate the sorority's meaning to one another. But, we know and truly believe you can change that.

Of course you should respect the sorority's esoteric rituals, ceremonies, and traditions; after all, they are an important part of your history. However, you also have to build your chapter's ability to communicate your core values through words and actions. To help clarify this point, consider the differences between your group's ceremony, ritual, and values. It is important to ensure we are working with the same definition of these three words. When the Eight Steps talk about communicating organizational values, it isn't meant to encourage your members to break their oath of secrecy about esoteric, ritualistic material. There is a distinct difference between the secret ceremonies of the sorority, the ritualized performance of those ceremonies, and the values that form the backbone of the organization.

At Phired Up, we define these words as follows:

Values	ideas, ideals, rules for living, principles
Ritual	actions, patterns of behavior, expressions
Ceremony	performance, event, play, theater, celebration

The words used to communicate the message(s) in the ceremonies are only one way to express the values of your sorority. In fact, those very ceremonies actually encourage you to communicate your values through your actions and your character. Even more than that, your ritualistic ceremonies encourage you to literally share the meaning of your organization with others, so that they might also find common values and join.

The ideals, principles, guiding statements, and rules of the organization, as identified and set in stone by the founders, are called *values*. A system for creating a way to commit to these values and communicate a consistent message was established and is called *ceremony*. Through the ceremony you express what should already be known to others from your behavior patterns. The hidden message of the ceremony which explains to new candidates the values that you live and act out on a daily basis is called *ritual*.

The decisions you make everyday in response to your values separate you from the masses. Hence the common saying, "live your ritual," which simply suggests, "live your values." The commitment to living your values is the foundation of your organization's past, present, and future. In a time when the public is always watching and the media is quick to provide headlines boasting misfortunes, administrators, parents, and students look with a critical eye at sororities and ask the question, "What value do you bring to our community?" Your ability, or inability, to perpetuate the timeless values of your ritual will determine your fate, be it prosperity or extinction.

The next time your chapter does membership selection and votes on who will have the opportunity to be your newest sisters, consider the fact that your organization's ritual probably did not demand that you were the most perfect candidate before you were allowed entry into its sacred walls. Most sororities are actually based on one simple criterion for membership: commitment. If someday, you get a chance to sit down with your ritual book (by the way, the lock on your ritual closet isn't there to keep *you* out), glance in there to see what commitments you have really made. You'll find out that all your sorority asks of its sisters during the new member process and during their membership is for a commitment to Achieving, Communicating, and Expecting the values of the organization.

Can the potential new member you are considering make that commitment? There are a few challenges, however, that come along with that seemingly simple commitment. First, you have to know that you're asking for that same commitment from all your sisters. Secondly, you have to communicate that commitment to potential new members before they join. And, thirdly, you have to actually live up to your end of the bargain; if one of your sisters breaks that commitment, you must hold them accountable for their actions.

Check out the next few pages for a few tools that will help you with this step!

Values-Based Selection Criteria

Does your chapter have a written set of criteria determining what to look for in a new member? Break away from the "she's so cute!" mentality and implement a "Values Based Selection Criteria." Display these criteria during rush events (potential members should know what you are looking for), use them to decide who is qualified to receive a bid, and make new members aware that they were chosen based on their achievements and character within these standards.

Values	Standards
_____	_____
_____	_____
_____	_____
_____	_____
_____	_____
_____	_____

Examples:

Academic Excellence   Has 3.0 or above

Community Service   Has a history of service, including 4+ hrs/ month last year

Friendship   Has a meaningful relationship with 3 sisters who can speak on her behalf.

Several organizations have a member commitment form, no more than one page in length, which outlines the commitments of every member and requires her signature every year. It serves as a reminder to keep our membership commitments fresh in our memory. In fact, we recommend checking with your national organization on this one, because a lot of them have this resource already created for you! Could your chapter benefit from a tool like this?

Member Commitments

What commitments do you ask of your members? What must each member agree to commit to in order to be your sister?

_____

_____

_____

_____

_____

_____

_____

_____

_____

_____

_____

_____

_____

_____

_____

_____

_____

_____

_____

Examples:

- *Pay your dues in full and on-time.*
- *Hold a leadership position in at least one other organization on campus.*
- *Attend weekly chapter meetings with prompt arrival.*

Values Case Studies

The following case studies are based on actual events; evaluate the situation, and assess the members' activities and decisions based on your core values as well as those of your sorority. Ask yourself the following questions: How will this situation support or compromise our core values? How will I react? Are my chapter's recruitment efforts (and other efforts) values-based? Pose these questions to your members and see how their responses differ.

- *April is the community service chair of your organization. She has been excited all semester about combining recruitment efforts with community service by holding an event during recruitment week that raises money to support the local Boys and Girls Club. At your chapter meeting, April stands up to announce that the chapter is sponsoring a "topless" carwash at a gas station on the edge of campus. The carwash is advertised as "topless," but when participants show up for the excitement, they are surprised by the twist that the top of their car will not be washed (and, of course, everyone will be keeping their shirts on). Another sorority did a similar event last semester and raised more than $1000 in just one day, plus they had a blast.*

- *Lindsay is a 5th year senior with the most experience in your chapter. She has a great idea for a new member activity that she did before she pledged. Lindsay comes to you with a list of 25 tasks that she will be challenging the chapter's new members to complete. The list includes some educational tasks, such as looking up questions on the chapter's history in the library and getting personal information from sisters. The list also includes some "adventures," as Lindsay referred to them, such as seeing how many men new members can kiss in one hour and stealing a composite picture from the fraternity your chapter is doing homecoming with.*

- *Your chapter is very well known on campus as the most beautiful and popular sorority around, and it is natural that you attract talented people. Tracy, a sophomore with a 3.8 GPA, is actively involved as a volunteer with Habitat for Humanity and was president of the freshman class. Tracy is friendly, outgoing, and incredibly excited about joining your organization. She seems like a great recruitment candidate, but she is also overweight. During membership selection, a sister speaks up stating that she is not sure Tracy "fits in with the image of your group."*

- *To show chapter unity and promote the organization's name, Grace, an art major, has designed "the coolest crush party t-shirts ever." The front displays the sorority letters and symbols. The back boasts a large picture of a peace sign with the text above it reading "Everyone wants a..."*

- *Anna is a great sister and a pretty good student. Last year, she took the same history class with the same professor that one of the chapter's new members, Tera, is taking. Tera's history midterm is tomorrow morning, so she tells the sisters she cannot join them at the Thursday night event with Alpha Alpha fraternity. Anna says, "Wait here," then returns a few minutes later with a copy of the midterm. She gives it to Tera and says, "Now there's no excuse for you not to come have a great time with us."*

- *One of the perks of being an upperclassman is having the option to live off campus. This year, two of the chapter's seniors, Esther and Annie, live in an amazing apartment where they often host parties for sisters and friends. Since you can't drink alcohol in your on-campus house, Esther comes to the rescue with the announcement that she and Annie will host unrestricted parties for sisters, friends, and potential new members to help get recruitment numbers up this semester.*

GO FOR IT, GIRL!

Experience the limitless possibilities that await your chapter right away by applying the ideas provided here:

♥ Does your chapter have a written set of criteria for a potential new member to receive a bid? Is it more than just being "so cute?" Get the chapter together and determine your values-based selection criteria.

♥ Are values important? Some sisters argue that the challenge of upholding your collective commitment to an agreed upon values system defines "sorority." Go find your ritual book and read it to understand what every sister has sworn to live by. Think about how that commitment affects the women you recruit.

♥ Schedule a debriefing session for ALL sisters after any new member ritual ceremony. Use this time to answer questions, discuss the ceremony, identify values, and talk about how/why the chapter exemplifies these founding beliefs.

♥ Use the case studies provided in this chapter to spark challenging, values-based discussions with your sisters.

S.P.A.M.

Hang in there, ladies, because this next question might make you a bit squeamish, but we promise this is going somewhere good. Have you ever had the opportunity of cracking open an ice cold can of meat? That's right, we're talking about the canned, spiced, mystery pork and ham by-product affectionately know as S.P.A.M. So, what comes to your mind when we mention S.P.A.M.? Go ahead; make your own list of words that you think of when you hear the term S.P.A.M. While you're at it, don't just think of the wonderful mystery meat, but also think about email S.P.A.M.

Typically, when we ask that question to a group of college students, we get the following answers:

Yuck

Disgusting

Fake

Annoying

Gelatinous Goo

Nasty

Mystery Meat

Cheap

Not Much Substance

Repetitive

Junk

What is it?

Stupid

A can of nothing
What do those letters mean anyway?
Worthless waste of my time
I think you can eat it, but you probably don't want to.
Delicious (there is always someone)
Obnoxious
I'd rather eat my arm
I guess it's technically food, but gross

Most people have a very clear opinion of S.P.A.M. and, most often, it's not a good one. Ironically, the overwhelming majority of people have never tried it. They just "know" it's not for them.

Now, here is a different question. Do you have anyone on your campus that is anti-Greek? We bet you are sitting there nodding your head and, maybe, you even have someone pictured in your mind. Here's a better question. Is it possible that a few of those words describing salty meat products and billions of annoying emails might be similar to words your anti-Greek classmates would use to describe the Greek organizations on your campus? Come on, we all know *you* might even describe some of your *fraternities* that way!

Go ahead and read the list again. We'll wait.

It's a fun analogy, but, sadly, one that works well. Some of the Greek organizations you'll encounter around the country (hello – fraternities) actually are rather disgusting, annoying, and a lot like canned meat, without much substance and put together in a mysterious box with strange letters on the front that nobody understands.

Now, look in the mirror ladies. It's easy and maybe even a little enjoyable to make fun of men, but we are just as bad. How many anti-Greeks do you know who might describe sororities as stupid, obnoxious, fake, annoying, cheap, worthless wastes of time, all living together in a mysterious box with strange letters on the front of it?

Pick your jaw up off the ground, because you know it is true. Keep reading. Now, consider how those anti-Greeks might describe your recruitment efforts: repetitive, in your face, strange, and annoying tactics to con people into joining something they don't actually want. Sounds a lot like email S.P.A.M., doesn't it? How many S.P.A.M. emails do you think people *actually* read? Very few, if any, right?

The truth is that the majority of people have never tried Greek life either, and their preconceived notion is that they "know" what it's all about and that it's not for them, without ever really trying it.

Anyway, it's just an analogy. The real lesson is the acronym that S.P.A.M. provides us. That acronym describes the reason for 95% of your sorority's recruitment problems (and, inevitably, organizational quality problems). Your recruitment results could dramatically increase with improvement in these four competencies: **S**kills, **P**roduct Knowledge, **A**udience Awareness, and **M**otivation.

With these four road blocks identified, we can get our arms around your recruitment problems and start addressing the real issues at hand. The reason that your chapter is not at its peak performance level is not because the administration is against you, another sorority uses dirty recruitment tactics, the college Panhellenic dropped the ball, you don't have a house, or any other excuse you can think of. These things are beyond your control and are typically a figment of your imagination anyway. They are excuses. They are the way you make yourselves feel better for not performing at top levels during recruitment.

The only reason you haven't dramatically increased the *quantity* of *quality* women in your chapter and community is because your members do not have the Skills, Product Knowledge, Audience Awareness, or Motivation necessary to succeed. These four things ARE within your control.

The 4 Competencies of Dynamic Recruitment

- **Skills:** Having the ability to communicate, socialize, and effectively grow your membership.

- **Product Knowledge**: Having a good understanding of your sorority, its value to members, and its value to the community.

- **Audience Awareness**: Having the awareness of who you want, where she is, and how to find her.

- **Motivation:** Having the drive and guts to do what is necessary to get the results you desire.

New Patterns of Behavior

Have you ever been driving in your car, gotten almost to your destination, and realized you have no idea what occurred during the last 10 minutes of the trip? Have you ever brushed your teeth without giving it any thought at all or tied your shoelaces without even looking? These are all tasks that took deep concentration and repetitive error when you first learned them. Now, however, you are doing them without thought. This is called a pattern of behavior.

Patterns of behavior are habits formed –voluntarily or involuntarily – from repetition. You can control a learned behavior, such as smoking cigarettes, just as you can control other behaviors, like reading a book before going to bed or shaking hands with strangers. How you make these a repetitive need in your life is up to you, but all can be learned and controlled. Patterns of behavior are present in your life all day, everyday, at your will. When you learn to take charge of these forces, you then begin taking hold of a powerful force in your daily life.

Psychologists have determined that it takes about 21 days to make or break a habit. In less than one month's time, you could employ new patterns of behavior in your life to transform sorority recruitment into a seamless part of your every day routine – just like tying your shoelaces. There is no need to spend all of your money and time on big recruitment events when they only return a handful of women. The Eight Step process empowers you to spread out the effort and spend a lot less money by implementing a system that incorporates the development of positive patterns of behavior in your members.

Patterns of behavior to improve your recruitment results start with reading this book, practicing the ideas in this book everyday for the next 21 days, teaching the ideas in this book to at least one other person, and then re-reading the book again to see what else you may have missed or can be inspired by.

We also provide new ideas to use as your patterns of behavior which will overcome your S.P.A.M. issues (lack of Skills, Product Knowledge, Audience awareness, and Motivation), but you have to commit to trying some of these new behaviors out and practicing them.   Let's start with Motivation.

"I've learned from experience that the greater part of our happiness or misery depends on our dispositions and not on our circumstances."

~Martha Washington~

STEP 3: GET MOTIVATED

Every chapter of every sorority, from their founding class to their alumnae group to their newest members, deals with motivation problems, especially when it comes to motivating members to actively do their part to recruit new people. Motivation is not something you fix in a moment; it's something you manage over time.

Theoretically, there are two types of people, those who are motivated intrinsically and those that are motivated extrinsically. Intrinsically motivated people are wonderful. They do things just for the joy of doing them and are able to motivate themselves to accomplish goals. Extrinsically motivated people often need to be pushed a little to do things. Most folks are motivated by reward, not punishment; by congratulations, not scolding; and by getting money, not by being fined. Women also want to feel that they are important to the functioning of your chapter, that they are a part of things, and that their membership is a part of the chapter's success.

The most important thing to understand about motivating others in a group is that most people will work as hard as their dream is important to them. In other words, they are motivated by *their* desires, not yours. To this end, there is something you can do to motivate your sisters to get fully involved in recruitment and to do their part to grow your organization to its fullest potential. Together, you can build a dream.

Have you ever had a dream? Not a daydream or a sleepy-time dream, but one of those dreams that made you believe that you would do anything possible to achieve it? Maybe you had the dream of making the soccer team while everyone around you said you weren't coordinated enough or too slow. Maybe you had the dream of attending a specific college, perhaps the one you are enrolled in now, but people around you said there was no way you could get admitted there or had enough money to attend. Maybe you had a dream of getting that totally awesome internship that everyone else said was a long shot.

You know what we mean. We're talking about a big, motivating, powerful dream that pulls you toward it; one that means so much to you that you would do anything within your means to achieve it.

What is your dream?

Do you know the individual dreams of your sisters?

A Lesson on Motivation

Stephanie hated recruitment. Every semester the Recruitment Chair would try to get everyone excited about these fake events where everyone acted all nice just to impress a bunch of freshmen. Anyway, Stephanie felt she wasn't very good at meeting new people and having chit-chat conversations.

Formal recruitment week was coming up and Stephanie was dreading it again. Her chapter was one of the smaller groups on campus and they sometimes fell short of recruiting who they actually wanted. She considered it to be the Recruitment Chair's job to recruit new girls and, even if she was supposed to help out, why should she bother? The chapter always did alright without her help and there just never seemed to be any point in trying.

Stephanie was sitting around with her big sister, Emma, one afternoon and they started talking about how awesome the upcoming homecoming week was going to be. They attended a Big 10 school and their football team was supposed to be incredible this year. Homecoming was a huge competition at their school in which all the Greek organizations were involved. Their chapter had not won homecoming in fifteen years, primarily because the competition was heavily weighted on "spirit points," which was code for "whoever can scream and chant the loudest." Since their chapter was not the largest, they never did as well as they wanted in this department. As they were talking about how much fun the tailgate parties were going to be, what they would be doing in the skit and dance competition, and how they were going to decorate their float, Stephanie had a thought...

"Wouldn't it be cool if we could actually win this year? Imagine if our chapter had about 200 women in it, and we all showed up to all of the events, screaming and cheering, and wearing the same T-shirt. We'd have a shot at winning for sure and probably get exposure in the local news. We certainly would gain more credibility as an organization, too."

"You know, Stephanie, all we'd have to do is have each sister meet, like, five or six people a day for a week. We could triple the size of our chapter, we just have to do it right," Emma replied.

Well, Stephanie had never considered that it might really be that simple and she had never imagined their chapter dominating the homecoming competition. How cool would that be? Maybe she would become a little more involved with recruiting new members this semester after all.

And the dream was started...

Does your organization have a dream right now? Does your chapter have something to shoot for? Do your members have a powerful, compelling reason to do the sometimes menial tasks it takes to make your recruitment efforts successful? Have you determined what, as a sorority, is important enough for all of you to work toward... so important, in fact, that it doesn't matter how much effort is necessary, it will get done?

There is a phenomenon in the sorority world called "Post-Chartering Blues." This happens when a newly chartered group has worked for a long time to achieve their status as a "chapter." Up to this point, all of the group's efforts have been focused on working to fulfill their dream of becoming an official chapter. Once all the pieces are in place and the group is officially chartered as a chapter, the "Post-Chartering Blues" set in. The group becomes apathetic, bored, and, typically, grows smaller. There is a chance that several members will drop out or lose touch with the chapter. Often, the group suddenly stops performing at its highest level.

Almost all new groups experience this and the cause is very simple. THE GROUP'S ONLY DREAM WAS TO BECOME A

CHARTERED CHAPTER. Once that dream was fulfilled, there was nothing else left to work for; there was no further MOTIVATION!

The reason for a chapter dream is obvious: you need something to work for. This is what drives your motivation. Once you've developed your dream in detail (the rest of this step can help you do that) and you know that you'll do whatever it takes to achieve that dream as a chapter, you'll find that your sisters will actually show up to events and activities, you'll find you have more volunteers, you'll find that your ladies will actually do what they said they would do, and they are more than happy to do all these things because the dream is as important to them as it is to you.

The funny thing about a sorority chapter dream is that almost every dream that any chapter can come up with is dependent upon one thing – recruitment. We'll let you figure that out for yourself, though. Start by building a dream, then see if you could have a much greater chance of achieving that dream (whatever it is) if you had a consistent, repeatable system to recruit a higher *quantity* of higher *quality* women.

Build Your Dream

Choosing to build your dream takes two key principles:

- There can be no limits on your dream. You must imagine a world of limitless possibilities.

- Choose a positive attitude. Choose an attitude of "Yes we can!"

Now, it is time to build your dream. Take some time for yourself right now to write down your own dream. There are some questions on the following pages to help you with this exercise. Once you've written down your personal dream, you've completed the first part of the process. Next, do this exercise with your entire chapter, with your new member classes, alumnae, and even with your potential members to see what it is that gets them motivated.

There will be no more excuses as to why your chapter women are not motivated to do their part in recruitment. You will have the power of the dream that you create to drive your efforts from here on forward.

To begin the exercise, start to imagine those late night conversations you've had with other members of your chapter. Remember those conversations? They start with: *"Wouldn't it be great if our chapter...."* Then, fill in the blank.

That's the beginning of a dream.

Now take it further.

Pull out a few blank sheets of paper and answer the following questions. Spend some time pushing yourself to brainstorm (remember, imagination has no limitations... you have limitless possibilities) through all of the details of your dream. The bigger the better. The more thorough the better.

What would your chapter be able to HAVE if it had as many high quality women as it wanted?

(Think about tangible things that you can touch.)

What would your chapter be able to DO because of those high quality women?

(Think about activities, trips, events, and other stuff you can do.)

What would your chapter BECOME as a result of having as many high quality women as it wanted?

(Think about how you will see yourself as a result of your fulfilled dream. How will others see you? What does your chapter become once your dream is achieved?)

A long time ago, a young woman had a dream to start your sorority. Just look what has happened since then!

What do you dream about? Are you brave enough to dream bigger and better than your contemporaries? Are you smart enough to share your dream with your sisters and write it down like your founders did?

Some people are really great at dreaming big. Other people might need a little more help. Try the following exercises with your chapter sisters to help build your dream to be as big as it can be.

- Take a road trip to the biggest chapter in your sorority at another college or university.

- Attend a national or regional sorority event.

- Find a sorority's chapter composite picture of a group that is twice as big as your chapter. Post a copy of it in your house or meeting area.

- Calculate what your chapter's budget could be if it had three times the members it has today.

- Calculate the service hours and philanthropic dollars that a chapter twice your current size could accumulate.

- Take a tour of a sorority house that holds 100+ women.

- Call your sorority's Inter/National headquarters and ask them to tell you about the biggest and best chapters in the country.

Eighteenth century British philosopher Jeremy Bentham first introduced the Pleasure/Pain Principle when he suggested that all people act in accordance with the pursuit of pleasure or the avoidance of pain.

Within the context of sorority, we can motivate ourselves and others by not only building big pleasurable dreams, but also by attaching exciting rewards and painful consequences to the actualization of those dreams.

As a recruitment example, a sister might choose you to be her accountability buddy. She might agree to introduce herself to five new women on campus a day for five consecutive days. She turns over her DVD collection to you – her accountability buddy – and may only reclaim it after the completion of her goal. You agree to celebrate when she achieves her goal by splitting a tub of rocky road ice cream and watching movies all night. The keys to making this form of motivation work are 1) a true and responsible friend to be the accountability buddy, 2) a worthwhile and attainable goal, 3) an exciting reward and/or painful consequence, and 4) checkpoints of progress along the way.

What do we do about chapter apathy?

The summer after graduation, three Panhellenic sisters, Margo, Robyn, and Melissa sat down at a local coffee shop for a little girl talk. Interestingly enough, the three women were all, at one point, involved with the same guy named Wes. Melissa had dated him her freshman year, Robyn as a sophomore, and Margo as a junior. The three girls actually bonded over their failed relationships with Wes when they were all seniors, having been through, what seemed like, some similar challenges with him.

"Wes has serious commitment and communication issues," cried Melissa. *"He actually broke out into a sweat when, after 8 months of dating, I wanted him to meet my Mom. I tried a million times to introduce him to her. I even staged a night when we would 'accidentally' run into her and he pretty much said hello and excused himself from the conversation to go out to the car. When I confronted him, he didn't even care. I knew then this was never going to go anywhere."*

"I know what you mean," said Robyn, *"Wes not only never met my parents after a year of dating, but instead of calling me about problems, he would always send me text messages to communicate important things to me. I would pick up the phone to call him and he wouldn't answer. When I confronted him about it, he would give some lame excuse, like he turned his phone on silent or he was in the other room, and make it seem like no big deal. What a jerk!"*

"You know, Wes is really not that bad. I ended up in a happy relationship during my junior year because of him," interrupted Margo.

"What?!" exclaimed Melissa. *"Are you serious? Didn't you have any of these problems with him?"*

"Well, yes I did. I found him to be quite apathetic and challenging. I couldn't get him to do anything that I wanted," said Margo.

"Then how can you say you ended up in a happy relationship during your junior year?" asked Robyn.

*"Well, after about 2 weeks, I realized that Wes was a total ass, so I dumped him for Joey, who is a complete **stallion**! Joey not only loves my family, but is also a great communicator."*

Maybe you've dated some asses or stallions like these women have. If not, maybe you've actually been to a farm and seen *real* asses (a.k.a. mules) and stallions (a.k.a. horses), and can understand the story from that experience. Here's a question: Have you ever tried to push a mule? What happens? They push back; and if you push a second time? They kick you in the face. You can never force a mule to do what you want them to do.

Well, just like the smelly farm animals, you can't change the mules (asses) that you've dated, nor can you change the mules in your chapter. Consider all of the time you invest in trying to motivate the mules in your chapter. Instead of spending all of your time getting kicked in the face by the mules (trying to get them to do what you want), use your time to recruit with your "horses". In a fraction of time, how many work horses could you personally recruit that would eagerly lead the chapter the way you do? Always leave the door open for your apathetic and challenging members; invite them to get more involved and praise them when they do. However, keep in mind that the best solution to your apathy problems is working with your smart, excited, passionate, and high quality members (horses) to recruit even more smart, excited, passionate, high quality members.

GO FOR IT, GIRL!

Experience the limitless possibilities that await your chapter right away by applying the ideas provided here:

♥ Spend an upcoming chapter meeting or retreat building your chapter's collective dream. Start by letting individual members build their own dreams. Then, do it collectively as a chapter to see what everyone wants to achieve together.

♥ Realize that each sister is motivated by something entirely unique. If you want to motivate your sisters, or just hold them accountable, ask them what the best way to do that is. Develop a spreadsheet of each sister's motivators based on their own individual recommendations.

♥ Use the "Have, Do, Become" exercise for everything you truly want to achieve (maybe a degree or a job) and post your written dream on your bathroom mirror for daily review. Harvard studies have shown this to be extremely powerful.

♥ Build recruitment teams of 2-5 sisters to support each other and serve as accountability partners for their other sisters.

How To?

The "How To?" Steps (4, 5, and 6) are about building the perspective, knowledge and capability to effectively share sorority life with the world. These Steps open your mind to your chapter's and community's potential, they provide practical methods for finding and getting to know potential members, and they refine your ability to communicate the value of your sorority to others who haven't yet experienced it. Push yourself to not only absorb the information in these chapters, but also practice using the new skills you learn to become a truly revolutionary recruiter.

"What you see depends mainly

on what you look for."

~unknown~

Step Four: Know your audience

You can't recruit who you don't know. Let us say that again. You can't recruit who you don't know. It's just like we've been saying – recruitment is not about cool skits, fancy themes, and drinks that correspond in color to the shirts you are wearing (yes, there are chapters that still do that and they know who they are). Recruitment is about building relationships with people outside your organization in an effort to find out who they are and eventually asking them to join.

The fact of the matter is that there are a lot more potential members out there on your campus who may be interested in joining a sorority than you probably know about. There are certainly more potential members out there on your campus than you actually *know*. A while back, some important researchers determined that, on average, most college campuses have three types of women that show up on the first day of their freshman year.

- **"Always Joiners."** Statistically, 15% of women report being "likely to join a sorority" when surveyed early in their freshmen year.

- **"Maybe Joiners."** Approximately 70% of the female population does not know or does not care a whole lot about sororities. They could be convinced to join if it was proposed the right way.

- **"Never Joiners."** An estimated 15% of the female population is adamantly opposed to joining Greek life. These sorority-haters would not accept a bid if it came with an SUV, a Prada bag, and a free cruise to the Bahamas.

So there is a unique population, about 70% of your non-affiliated women on campus to be exact, who don't really know about sorority life. These women do not have family members already in Greek organizations, they may be first generation college students, or they just might not know what sorority life is really all about. THIS IS YOUR MOST IMPORTANT GROUP. Most of these women don't join sororities simply because no one has EVER approached them with the idea. These women are not going to actively seek out information about sororities and they aren't going to come to your formal recruitment events (because they think that stuff is kind of weird). YOU HAVE TO GO TO THEM! They aren't going to come to a recruitment event or sign up for recruitment based on some flier or mass-email. These are the people you, your chapter members, and your council have to actively recruit.

So, we've got this special group of people. Remember that percentage (70%) because we'll use it in a minute. And it's probably worth mentioning that you might be a lot like one of the authors of this book, Jessica. When she showed up at college, she said, "There's no way I'm ever joining one of those snobby sororities. Sororities = not me." Now she's writing a book about sorority recruitment. While she thought she was a "Never Joiner," she was actually a "Maybe Joiner," but she just didn't know it.

Before you can talk about how to recruit those 70% of "Maybe Joiners" into your organization, you need to understand who they are and how you find them.

Alright, time for some math.

Who loves math? You? Great! Then, you'll really enjoy this next exercise we've provided for you. We know you can handle this because that silly rumor that "girls aren't good at math" is just a myth some man created to feel superior. Trust us, this is easy.

Take out your pencil and calculator, and try the equation found on the next two pages out for size. The equation goes something like this:

Current Student Body – Current Panhellenic Women – Men – Never Joiners =
Potential New Member Pool

Ok, here we go:

1. Write down the population of your undergraduate student body on Line A

2. Subtract the number of male students from your student body population, and put the number of females on Line B.

3. Great! Now, subtract the number of women already in sororities on your campus from Line B, and put the answer on Line C.

4. Great! Now, from Line C, subtract 15% (**"Never Joiners"**), and write that new number on Line D.

_____ Line A

-_____ Number of Male Students

_____ Line B

-_____ Number of Women already in Sororities

_____ Line C

-_____ 15% of Line C

_____ Line D

Line D is the realistic prospective membership pool on your campus. Now, do a little more math (we told you this was a good time) and take another 15% off of Line D ("Always Joiners"). That number is the TOTAL untapped resource of potential members on your campus. Think about it.

What we are trying to get at is that there is this totally untapped resource on your campus that no one is using. There are a vast amount of women, who, if the right person approached them in the right way about sorority life, might genuinely be interested. In this part of the book, we want to not only raise your awareness of your chapter and community's potential, but also show you some useful ways to reach those women, get their names, and start talking to them about sorority life on your campus with the hope that even half of your "Maybe Joiner" population would be interested (still a pretty big number, huh?).

I am sure you have heard of the phrase, "We're about *quality* not *quantity*," right? In the sorority world, it's typically what we say to make ourselves feel better for not performing well during recruitment. Well, at Phired Up we believe in a different phrase, "*quantity* drives *quality*." Now, we're not saying go and hand out bids to all of the "Maybe Joiners" on your campus. We are saying that the higher *quantity* of women you have in the recruitment process the higher *quality* of women you can recruit to join your organization. The battle is reaching the population of "Maybe Joiners," getting them interested in sorority life, and getting to know them so that you have the largest possible pool of people from which to choose *quality* members.

So, how do you find those people? That's a great question.

Mind Joggers

The first and most important step is to develop a list of names, contact information, and basic information about *as many potential members as possible.* We'll call this a "Names List." It is important to note that a Names List is different than a list of the top girls you'd really like to recruit from your campus. This is what some chapters might call a Names List, but it is really a Wish List. There is a big difference.

Your Names List is the critical first step in developing a successful recruitment process. The larger your list gets, the more successful you will become. The first job of a chapter that practices *Dynamic Recruitment* is to create a Names List as large as possible. You will have the ability to recruit more *quality* individuals when you increase the size of your potential membership pool, thus maximizing your possibilities! You can put anyone and everyone on the Names List!

Here is how it's done:

Write down every unaffiliated woman you know on the Names List. DO NOT PREJUDGE ANYONE. Put everyone on the list. Now is **not** the time to decide if someone is qualified for membership. Pull out a big piece of paper (or create a simple computer spreadsheet) and get ready to write down all of the names you can think of. You can even use the space at the end of this book to start your Names List. Take a couple of minutes now.

Nice job! Most people are able to write down 10-20 names of non-Greek undergraduate women they know in the first minute or two. Now we'd like to challenge you – and the rest of your members – to jog your memory a little and think of all the non-Greek ladies you know, but may have forgotten to put on the list you just created. In fact, we're challenging you to expand your list to 50+ names. Sound like a lot? To help you do that RIGHT NOW, we've provided you a list of Mind Joggers. You can use these prompts to help ensure that you have exhausted your options. These will help you recall most of the names you have forgotten to include. Go for it, girl!

Write down all the non-Greek women you know who…

- Are scholars
- Are loyal
- Have good manners
- Are leaders on campus
- Are service minded
- Want to succeed in life
- Value family and friends
- Make you laugh
- Were/are on your freshman hall (all of them)
- Live on your floor or in the building
- Are on your sports team (all of them)
- Are on your intramurals team

- Are in the same clubs/organizations you are (get a roster)

- Exemplify pride in your school

- Current/past R.A.'s on campus

- Work with you at your job(s)

- Spend their time in the computer lab

- Spend their time in the library

- Are spiritually driven

- Sit with you at lunch/dinner … sit near you at lunch/dinner

- Sit within 10 seats of you in class

  o (do this for every class)

- Were in last semester's classes

- Are already an officer for another group on campus

- You've seen in the gym/weight room

- Always sit in the front/back of the class

- Have traveled abroad

- Withdrew or was released from formal recruitment

- Did not get accepted into/dropped out of another sorority

Now check the following resources for additional names:

- Your cell phone speed dial listing

- Address book/Palm Pilot/Buddy List

- Student directory/email/list serves

- List of all freshman females (from admissions office/student affairs)

- Rosters for clubs and organizations

- PHC sign up sheets (past years as well)

- Last year's yearbook

- Housing lists

- Rosters for sports teams

- Invitation lists from socials & formals

- Email lists/list serves

Women you may not have considered:

- Adult students

- Your freshman year RA

- Graduate students

- ROTC cadets

- International students

- That girl who never leaves her room

- University professionals/staff

- Your closest friend's friends

- Seniors you know

Did you get to 50? More? Well done! Regardless of how many names you got, it's still more names than you had before. This activity should be repeated at least once every semester with the entire chapter. The new member class should do this as soon as they begin the membership process. When done as a group activity, this may take 15-20 minutes.

Once you have each member's individual list of names, the information is compiled and added to the chapter's Names List. Congratulations, you just started your recruitment efforts with connections to hundreds (maybe even thousands) of potential new members.

Now, here is another novel idea, what if you did this activity as a Panhellenic Council, not just a sorority chapter? How cool would that be? More people equals more ideas for names, and you are increasing the *quality* and *quantity* of potential new members for everyone. Therefore, you are directly and dynamically impacting *the* Greek experience on your campus, not just *your* Greek experience (that's quite revolutionary!)

Shopping for Names

Just in case you haven't heard it enough yet, here's one more reminder: You can't recruit who you don't know.

There is a lot to recruiting a potential sister, and we'll get to all of that, but it is absolutely true that you just plain can't recruit who you don't know (or maybe you could, but that wouldn't get the *quality* results you are looking for.) Later in the book (Step Six), we will show you how to specifically meet people and carry on a normal conversation, but before you make contact with those people, you need a mechanism to keep track of all of the names you are going to be collecting.

Remember, that's what we call a Names List. A Names List is simply a way that you keep track of the women that you have made contact with or that you have gotten contact information for and plan on contacting. You can use a spreadsheet, a bed sheet, or a big piece of paper on the wall (we recommend Microsoft Excel™). You store their name, where they live, their phone number, email address, how you got their name, who met them, and any other identifiable information. This way you can better keep track of your recruitment efforts.

So, here are five ways that you can get NAMES. That's all we're talking about here. We need to get the names of as many people as possible on a list. From there, we can work on building the relationship and, maybe, if all the stars align, we can ask some of them to join. But, first, we simply need to get a ton of names on a list.

We've said it before and we'll say it again: *quantity* drives *quality*. The more women you get to know and the more names you can accumulate, the better chance you'll have of getting more high *quality* members.

There are five ways to maximize your list of potential member names. We like to equate this to one of our favorite pastimes – shoe shopping! That's right sisters, we think shoe shopping is just about one of the most amazing things in the world! Maybe you don't, and that's cool, but just bear with us on the girly examples!

Shoes are marvelous and shopping for them can be a blast, most of the time. Sometimes your dreams of new shoes are thwarted because you look down at the enormous price tag, have a rude sales lady, the store doesn't have the pair you want in your size, or you have to wait in line forever to purchase them! The best thing about shoe shopping (and shopping in general) is that you always have plenty of options. So, maybe it isn't in the budget this month to get those killer BCBG pumps; Target has a pair that is pretty similar and way cheaper.

You can always go to that one big department store for shoes, but you'll probably limit your selection and may have to deal with a rude sales person or, worse, a crowd of 1,000 other women pining over the same shoes that you want. So, instead of just limiting yourself to the rush of the big department store, you might empower yourself with deals from the newspaper, a little Internet shopping, a trip to Kohl's, a visit to a friend who works in a shoe boutique, or a recommendation from someone who has killer shoes. There are plenty of different ways to find the best pair of shoes for you, so why limit yourself to just one option?

Sound familiar? We thought so. Only participating in one of the "5 Secrets of Shopping for Names" is just like limiting yourself to shoe shopping at only one store. The main idea of the 5 Secrets is that you could rely on just one of them, like formal recruitment, but that would only be 1/5th of your potential. You need to use all 5 in order to maximize your potential. If you want to engage more women in formal recruitment, you need to use the other four secrets as well. Furthermore, and most importantly, the ONLY way to grow your community is to first meet a lot more people – get them on your Names List – and these are the *five* ways to do just that.

> **The 5 Secrets of Shopping For Names:**
> 1. Referrals
> 2. Member Positioning
> 3. Names Drives
> 4. Marketing for Names
> 5. Formal Recruitment

1. Referrals - *Think of all the places that sell shoes.*

When shoe shopping, you want to ask a lot of people where the best places are to buy shoes. Chances are that everyone will have a different opinion, thus giving you a lot of ideas. The same goes for getting names for your Names List. You should ask for referrals from a ton of different people in order to gain as many names as possible.

Begin by using the "Mind Joggers" activity that we have provided at the end of the chapter to get referrals from yourself and your members. The average member can generate about 50 names with very little effort. When the activity is done in three minutes, most women can produce at least 10 names. The Mind Jogger activity should be done in about 20 minutes.

With referrals, you can also specifically ask people to refer women who they think would be a good sorority woman. Ask for referrals of top undergraduates from fraternity leaders, faculty and staff members, administrators, alumnae, parents, and other campus organization leaders. Also consider using technology with websites that link new friends together (MySpace, Facebook, Friendster, LinkedIn, etc.) Additionally, check into names of individuals that graduated from your high school or a high school near you and solicit referrals from there.

2. Member Positioning - *Kathy works at Saks Shoe Department and gets an awesome discount.*

Saks has a pretty awesome shoe selection, so it only makes sense to know someone who works there so you have the insider information on all the best deals and discounts. The same goes for getting names; if you want the best members and leaders on campus, you have to recruit from where the best leaders on campus are. Every member of your chapter should be involved in multiple campus organizations and leadership roles. Encourage and recommend chapter members to get involved in residence life as an RA, through admissions work, orientation programs, campus tours, recreation center/intramurals, honorary organizations, student government, and so forth. Use rosters and contact sheets from those organizations to build your Names List.

3. Names Drives - *I am taking a poll of all of the stylish women I know: Where did you get those adorable shoes?*

There are many different ways to find potential new members throughout the year, just like there are many different ways to find shoes. When you are looking for some great shoes, one of the ways to find them is to ask other people where they got theirs – an easy activity that helps you find great shoes. Name Drives are activities that produce names for your Names List. Some such activities include recruitment pushes, move-in days, information tables, and cold calling.

Our favorite way is called, "5 for 5." "5 for 5" is simple, not to mention it's one of the most effective ways we've found to dramatically increase your Names List. If you do "5 for 5," there is a good chance you'll get more women through this effort than you've ever gotten from formal recruitment.

"5 for 5" is a challenge. Are you willing to meet, just meet, 5 new women a day for the next 5 days? If you are willing to take on that challenge and make that commitment, you alone can grow your sorority's potential membership pool by 25 people. If 4 of your sisters take that challenge with you, then your chapter will grow its Names List by 125 people within only 5 days. How many of your formal recruitment events have ever resulted in personal conversations with 100+ women? Start "5 for 5" today.

4. Marketing for Names - *I got information from my friend via email about bidding on an awesome pair of shoes on eBay.*

The important thing to remember about marketing is that it can promote positive public relations; but, if it doesn't produce names, then you don't really get any results. In shoe terms, it's just like all of those shoe ads that you see in magazines – if they don't help you find the perfect shoes, what good are they? Some of you may be scratching your head. Yes, we said, "marketing" and "producing names" in the same sentence. You should market your chapter in ways that will also produce names. Consider promoting academic scholarships, hosting a banquet, sports league involvement, soliciting involvement for a service project, parent solicitations, and so forth. What do people typically give you when you ask them to participate in something like that? Yeah, now you're getting it. That's right, CONTACT INFORMATION! And, bingo, more names!

5. Formal Recruitment - *I am just going to run down to the mall and pick up some shoes; that is the easiest thing to do.*

When you are looking for a pair of shoes, the easiest and most familiar thing to do is to run down to the mall and find a pair. However, that may not always produce the best results. You might not always find that *perfect* pair of shoes.

Likewise, traditional "formal recruitment" is one of the most common and familiar methods used by sororities to find new members. You should participate in the programming and maximize its potential, but also realize that you are reaching only a limited percentage of your potential pool during traditional, formal recruitment, just like if you only went to the mall looking for shoes.

As you build your Names List and begin to make contact with the women on your list, chances are that some of these women will go through your sorority's formal recruitment process (fully, partially, or minimally structured). Building your Names List prior to recruitment will help your chapter maximize your recruitment potential during the formal process. While most traditional "formal recruitments" are what we call *static*, there are many ways to use formal recruitment as a part of your chapter or community's *Dynamic Recruitment* system.

What chapters and communities must realize through the formal recruitment process is that there are women who withdraw or are released from the formal recruitment process, but who are still very interested in being Greek and would make great new members. So, remember to gather these names throughout the process. Ask your Greek advisor for a list and don't forget to revisit last year's formal recruitment list for quality women who have not yet joined a sorority.

Furthermore, you are going to have amazing and exciting new members once this process is complete. Use them to build your Names List. No one knows more freshman than other freshman, so capitalize on their excitement for names!

Just a quick P.S. It would be a REALLY good idea to teach your newest members about your newfound *Dynamic Recruitment* knowledge. As you continue to learn, begin teaching them! By the time they are seniors, your chapter will be full of members that have never known the old *Static Recruitment* ways.

Whatever methods you end up using to build your Names List, Step 4 is really about seeing your chapter's potential and shifting your efforts to build as many personal relationships as possible with the women on your campus. Success, beyond your expectations, is available right now. And that's without even mentioning the non-traditional members that could join your organization if asked: graduate students, professors, university staff members, community leaders, your members' mothers, campus religious leaders, and many others.

Remember: You can't recruit who you don't know. Now, open your eyes to your limitless potential and choose to see the possibilities! By the way, you get extra points for wearing spectacular shoes while you go for it, girl!

GO FOR IT, GIRL

Experience the limitless possibilities that await your chapter right away by applying the ideas provided here:

- ♥ Calculate the number of potential members at your school with the math equation provided earlier in this book. Once your chapter members see the potential, teach them about the "5 Secrets of Shopping for Names" and how to reach those "Maybe Joiners."

- ♥ Make a 5 day growth plan with 4 of your best friends in the sorority. Together, commit to "5 for 5" and use one another to hold each other accountable for the growth plan (don't forget about what motivates each one of you). Determine some fraternity men, classmates, professors, staff, and others from whom you could ask for referrals. Run through the Mind Joggers and figure out all the other small ways you could grow your chapter's Names List in just 5 days.

- ♥ Start a real Names List. Develop a spreadsheet using your favorite database software (Microsoft Excel® is fine), and include a column for names, phone numbers, Email addresses, notes, and etc. You can find an example of a Names List online at: http://www.PhiredUp.com/

♥ Empower your new members to start adding to the Names List right away. They have different networks than your chapter members.

♥ Write down your plan for next year's recruitment using the "5 Secrets." Remember not to limit yourself to just one department store – plan for a shopping spree of success!

♥ Begin to work lessons about *Dynamic Recruitment* into your new member education program.

"A strong, positive self-image is the best possible preparation for success."

~Joyce Brothers~

STEP 5: KNOW YOUR PRODUCT

Step Five is a simple sales tip spun slightly to fit within our sorority scope. We know, some of you are thinking, *"I'm not a saleswoman! Selling is so fake!"* Understand, though, that "selling" your sorority is actually helping other women obtain what could be the most meaningful experience of their lives – think of it more like charity (*you* are doing *them* a favor), than like used car sales or those annoying perfume ladies in the mall.

Knowing Your Product is about understanding the value that your organization adds to the lives of its members and the value that your organization adds to your community. Today's student wants to know how being a part of an organization is going to benefit them prior to joining – whether it be academically, socially, in future job searches, or otherwise. Step Five is about finding out what those benefits are, what value your chapter or community offers, and teaching your members how to effectively communicate those things to potential members. Without the ability to communicate those things, your chapter will be hard pressed to recruit the *quality* members you are seeking.

Step 5, the Know Your Product step, reminds us of a story we once heard. It's about a door-to-door makeup saleswoman named Jennifer.

Jennifer had just started her job as a makeup saleswoman and, so far, no one had answered their doors when she had knocked. People were avoiding her like it was their job. Finally, it looked like she might just get lucky with the next house on her route. She could hear the sound of music coming from inside and there was a car in the driveway.

Jennifer rang the doorbell. A few moments later, a young woman clumsily opened the door and greeted her with a kind smile that hid a frustrated, furled brow. She was dressed in her bathrobe with her hair in a bun on top of her head. It was obvious she had been washing her face.

"Hi there," the woman said. "Excuse my appearance, I have an important party to go to and my skin looks awful. I've put my make-up on three different times and I still look like crap. How can I help you?"

Well, obviously, Jennifer had hit the jackpot. So, she sprung into action. "Ma'am, you can't really help me, but I'm here to help you. I sell makeup, and I have just the thing to make your skin look beautiful and flawless."

"Really?" she asked with interest. "Obviously, I'm a lady in need of your services, but I'll need to know a little about this makeup first. You have my attention."

Keep in mind this was Jennifer's first time and she hadn't prepared quite as much as maybe she should have. "Ma'am, well... uhh... as you can see here, the makeup I have to sell you is... uh... well, it's foundation. And... uhh... well, it's like smelly, I mean not smelly, well it smells, but…it's like really good. It…uhhh…comes in this really cool bottle."

And that's the end of the story. Hey, we never said it was a good one. But, we still might be able to learn a valuable lesson from our young saleswoman. Jennifer wasn't prepared and when she had the opportunity to really sell her product, she blew it. Not only did that woman not buy Jennifer's makeup, but she probably won't ever buy makeup from any saleswoman that rings her doorbell again.

The moral of the story? If you don't know your product, you're probably not going to be able to sell it. In our sorority context, if you don't know how to "sell" your sorority, you'll probably have a very hard time convincing people to join it – even those who need it most.

Imagine for a moment that you are in an elevator within a very tall building on your campus. You're all alone in that elevator until, right at the last second, another woman steps in on your way down to the first floor. The woman who just jumped on the elevator with you happens to be the one woman on campus that you think exemplifies what a perfect sister in your sorority would be like; except, none of your sisters really know her well and you've never really hung out with her. You've always assumed she wasn't interested in joining a sorority.

This woman is President of three organizations on campus (including the student government), she's extremely popular, great at sports, is on the Dean's List, and she's just an all-around *classy lady*.

So, there you are on the elevator, with about 30 seconds until you reach the bottom floor, when she says, *"Hey, you're in that sorority right? Tell me, what's that all about?"*

Quick, what's your response?

If you said something like, *"Well... uhh... we're the pink house on the corner, and we have the cutest girls on campus, and... um ...we are like such a cool group,"* you might as well have been our saleswoman, Jennifer, exclaiming how her product is smelly and *"comes in a really cool bottle."*

There is one major question that Step 5 asks:

Can you help a potential member see how membership in the sorority will make *her* life better? (This means knowing how to communicate the *VALUE* of your organization.)

We talk a lot about "values" in the plural sense in the fraternity/sorority world, but, unfortunately, we don't often talk about just pure value. What value do you offer your members? What value does your organization offer you? Why is it worth the investment of time, energy, passion, and money to join your organization? What is the ROI (return on investment)?

If you start to answer those questions with statements like, *"We've won Greek Sing three years in a row,"* or *"We've got the nicest house on campus,"* or *"We do all sorts of service and philanthropy work,"* or even, *"We have the strongest sisterhood on campus,"* then we've got bad news for you. That's not going to be worth the investment for most potential members. That's not why they will join.

First of all, every one of those statements, including the ones that sound similar to it, is exactly what every other sorority on your campus is saying. Secondly, those statements are explaining the features of membership, and people don't invest their time, money, energy, or passion into *features*. People invest in the *benefits* of membership that your organization can provide to them in the short and/or long term.

Features are the things that you do as a sorority (philanthropy, intramurals, socials, etc.), as well as some of the superficial parts of the sorority experience (awards, accolades, t-shirts). So, yes, features are important to your chapter. They are things that are a part of the sorority experience in your mind, but most potential members don't necessarily care about those things (until they're actual members).

The benefits of your sorority go much deeper than features. A benefit shows a potential member how they will specifically benefit from being a part of your organization. Sure, your organization has philanthropic events, but potential members need to be shown that philanthropic events make you feel amazing by coming together as a group to get involved in the community and support local families that can use your help. Benefits are the ways in which the features of your organization will specifically add value to their lives, their experience, and their future. Benefits are not tangible, but are felt and lived through experiences.

The difference between a feature and a benefit can seem a little fuzzy sometimes. It might help to refer back to our friend Jennifer, the make-up saleswoman. If she had mentioned that her makeup was tan, it smells good, and it comes in a cool bottle, she would have been explaining the features of her product (all superficial descriptions – meaning the outward characteristics that all makeup has). The nice young lady wasn't looking for something that was tan, smelled good, or was in a cool package, she was looking for something to make her skin more beautiful. To help Jennifer explain the benefits instead of the features of her product, we might encourage her to mention that it makes skin more radiant, reduces wrinkles, tightens pores, and prevents against future skin break-outs.

This brings up another excellent point about Knowing Your Product: the value of the product is directly dependent upon the needs of your customer. The nice lady was looking for something that would help her skin, so even if Jennifer had explained ALL of the *benefits* of her product, the customer still only cared that it was going to make her skin more beautiful. Those were her needs.

You can regurgitate the benefits of membership in your organization or community to all 70% of the "Maybe Joiners" on your campus and each of them will hear different things or be interested for different reasons. Bottom line: people join for their own reasons, not yours. So, before you start sharing all of the wonderful benefits of being a member in your sorority, you should find out what she is looking for in an organization or group of friends. After that, you can help her see how your organization or community will benefit *her* in the ways she is looking to benefit.

For example:

Potential Member says, *"My family is really far away and I don't get to go home very much. I really want more friends and to find a place to call my home away from home."*

Sister Sorority says: *"Well, membership in a sorority allows you to form lifelong bonds of friendship with a core group of women you have an instant connection with. We have a chapter house that is awesome. Our members hang out there, study there, and we eat meals together at the house a lot, too."*

So, the next time you have an informal recruitment event or even one of those all-Greek events on campus (the ones where you publicly and proudly display your Greek Week trophies, photo albums, and banners on one of those super cool folding tables while talking to people about your sisterhood and philanthropies), ask yourself if you are focusing on the "features" or the "benefits" of your membership. If you tell a passerby about your great house, or about the large number of socials you have, you're explaining features. They won't invest their time into those features, because they're important to you, not them. Also, remember to ask them what *they* want to get out of their experience or what they are looking for, then help them to see how your organization or community will *benefit* them in those areas.

Excuses, Excuses

The other important task to accomplish in Step 5 is to learn how to handle excuses. You've got to know your product well enough to be able to get around all those excuses which inevitably pop up when asking your potential members to join.

You know what the excuses will be for not joining your sorority. They're the same every semester. What you need to do is be prepared with a surefire way to get past these excuses.

Top 10 Excuses for Not Joining a Sorority

1. I can't afford it.
2. My parents don't want me to join.
3. I've got to focus on my studies.
4. Upperclassmen don't join sororities.
5. I don't want to live in a sorority house.
6. I don't want to be one of those "stereotypical sorority girls."
7. I don't have the time.
8. I've got other friends already.
9. I don't want to buy my friends.
10. I don't want to get hazed.

Feel * Felt * Found. These three little words will guide your honest, authentic, quality responses and provide a framework for handling these excuses in the future.

Take one of the most common excuses, for example. *"I don't have the time; I really need to focus on my studies."*

You might respond: *"I know how you **feel**. I **felt** the same way before I joined. I was really scared by the time commitment. I had heard from all of my friends on other campuses that there is always so much going on in a sorority. I was nervous about keeping up my GPA and having time for my off-campus job. What I **found**, however, was that these women are actually really understanding. They want me to balance my sorority commitment with the rest of my life. We work really hard to encourage our members to put academics first and we understand if you can't make it to something because of other commitments. In our new member education program, we have a whole lesson on keeping a healthy life/work balance, and we have an amazing academic initiatives program with older sisters who tutor and mentor our new members."*

It is important to tell the truth in your response and to speak from your own experiences. Now just think, if you can prepare every member of your chapter with those three words, and they all practice and prepare to combat these excuses, wouldn't you be able to hang on to a lot more potential new members?

No doubt you'll encounter excuses like these. But, be prepared to get to the heart of the potential new member's concerns by using quality responses. Remember Feel * Felt * Found. You'll be amazed at the results.

Step 5 is simple. Understand the value that your sorority has to offer and be well prepared to be able to share that message with anyone who wants to hear about it.

Quality Responses

Quality responses are the ways in which you and your chapter members respond to the common excuses used to not join a sorority. When dealing with common excuses, it is important to use the words Feel*Felt*Found as your guide. However, many times people are so uncomfortable dealing with excuses they make several common mistakes:

- **Lying or half-truths**: Don't lie or even tell half a lie to potential members!

- **Dismissing:** It's a valid concern if it makes them concerned. Don't ignore it or suggest that it's not an issue. Explain it!

- **Failure to Listen:** Make sure you understand their needs and concerns before you start telling them *your* autobiography.

The ideal way to answer excuses is by facilitating a conversation with good follow-up questions, so that *she* can come to the conclusion, on her own, that the concern is not something that should keep her from joining a sorority. On the following page you will see some examples of questions you can use to create your quality response. Notice that we didn't try to immediately answer their concern. Rather, we ask follow up questions to better understand their concerns and lead them toward a realization that their concern might actually be a reason to join.

Quality Response Examples

I don't want to get hazed.

- Hazing is unacceptable and strictly forbidden in our sorority.
- Let me introduce you to our newest initiates. Feel free to ask them about any details of their new member period.
- Here is our new member education program outlining everything we do.

I can't afford it.

- Do you know how much it costs?
- May I show you exactly how much it costs and how that compares to other college expenses?
- If we could arrange a payment plan, would that make a difference?

My parents don't want me to join.

- What is it they do not approve of?
- Why do you think they feel that way?
- Have they met any of the members in this sorority?
- Would you be willing to help me arrange an opportunity for them to meet some of the members/members' parents?

I've got to focus on my studies.

- What are your concerns?
- Did you know the chapter has minimum standards for maintaining membership in the organization, an academic excellence program, and a program to reward scholastic achievement?
- May I introduce you to our scholarship chairman?

I am not one of those stereotypical sorority girls.

- What makes you think you would be a stereotype?
- What exactly are the stereotypes that come to mind?
- Does that accurately describe me and the girls you've met from our sorority?

GO FOR IT, GIRL!

Experience the limitless possibilities that await your chapter right away by applying the ideas provided here:

♥ Build your chapter's "Elevator Pitch." In 30 seconds, can you verbalize the *value* and *benefits* of being a member of your sorority?

♥ Read through your chapter's website, brochures, T-shirts, and any other written materials to make sure that they refer to the *benefits* of membership, not just the *features*.

♥ Prepare quality responses to the Top 10 Excuses for not joining (try putting them on flashcards). Make sure all of your members do the same, and then practice them together regularly. Try role-playing at the beginning or the end of chapter meetings for practice. You already have everyone in the room anyway, right?

♥ Remember back when you told your parents and other special family members about joining the sorority. How did you explain it to them? Often, that's the best way to explain it to others.

"The first problem for all of us, men and women, is not to learn, but to unlearn."

~Gloria Steinem~

STEP 6: DEVELOP SKILLS

Warning! You are embarking on the longest and most information laden section of the book, but it is also one of the most important. In this section, we are going to work on your people skills. Don't be scared, because this won't hurt a bit – just be prepared to take in A LOT of information. Sororities that have a *Dynamic Recruitment* process have great skills – skills that they continue to fine tune and practice. We are going to show you the skills you need to have to be successful in recruitment.

Women Only Join Sororities that Have Skills

First of all, you probably already know that the best women (and potential new members) on your campus are not going to approach you about joining a sorority. That's just not the reality of the situation. You might be wondering, "Well, then how in the heck do I meet them?" Have no fear, we are here to help you with that! This step, if practiced, can magically transform your members into recruitment machines by teaching them basic people skills along with advanced techniques to take your chapter's recruitment to the next level. Remember, the more people you meet, the better off you will be.

Meeting People Skills

OK, so you need some skills. The first and most basic of these skills are the "Meeting People Skills." Let's start there. We'll kick things off with a magic trick. Did you know that you can make anyone in the world focus all of their attention on you, offer up their full name, and reveal critical information at your will with one simple little trick? All you have to do is look at them, walk within four feet of where they are, and stick out your right hand (sorry lefties, this is a right-handed thing). Next, say the magic words, "Hi, I'm Susie Sorority." (Substitute your own name for maximum effect.) Then, by some unknown and possibly mystical force, the other girl will shake your hand and tell you her name. PRESTO! You have begun a personal conversation with this person and now the information will start to pour out of her mouth.

Slightly ridiculous and over the top? Yeah, maybe a little, but this is the single most effective skill of top performing politicians, salespersons, philanthropists, journalists, and even professional recruiters. Now, we realize that it isn't much of a "magic trick," but it is the single best way to meet someone new. After all, that is exactly what we are interested in during the early stages of recruitment. We aren't trying to dazzle people into joining (or even discussing the sorority, for that matter). All we want to do is find out whether or not the person on whom you have just preformed magic is worth getting to know better. All of that can be accomplished by having a basic conversation with her.

Once you have introduced yourselves to one another, you are no longer strangers, so loosen up and get to chatting! You may, however, need a few good kick off lines to get the conversation rolling. Here are a few options:

- Comment on something she is wearing, carrying, or doing.
  "I see you're wearing a Dance Marathon t-shirt. Did you participate last year?"

- Comment on a current or upcoming event that you may have in common.
  "Did you attend the concert on campus this past weekend?"

- Ask for assistance with something you are doing or for somewhere you are going.
  "I am looking for a few more volunteers to help a group raise money for a local humane society. Do you know anyone that might be interested in something like that?"

- Comment on an event you are hosting.
  "Did you hear about our Habitat for Humanity Sisterhood build? We are looking for a few more women to join us." OR *"We are hosting an event at the local pizza place tonight. The food is free and the band is awesome, you should stop by."*

The Most Important Word

Now, before we go much further, we have a quick question. Have you ever met someone for the second or third time, been interested in getting to know more about him or her, but you couldn't remember their name? It happens all the time. You'll meet someone (especially if it's someone you're interested in), you'll introduce yourself, and immediately your mind will wander off to what you're going to say next so that you can seem engaging. The problem is that we often never hear the other person's name and, by the time we realize this snafu, it is too late to do anything about it.

So, when you're out there making friends, don't forget that *her* name is the most important word in *her* vocabulary. Learning that one single word will make all the difference in the world to her. She will remember that you remembered her name because, as sad as it is, it is a pretty uncommon occurrence these days (and most other sorority chapters will be so focused on their skit, costumes, and decorations that you'll have a huge advantage). Invest your energy and concentration into memorizing her name.

Here's the best way to do that. After she says her name, repeat it in your next sentence, think of it again in your head, associate it with something about her (to help it "stick"), and then use it again when you say good-bye. For example, maybe you meet a red-haired girl named Ruby. You might say to yourself, "ruby red," to help you remember her name.

You might be saying, "Yeah right, I would never just walk up to a perfect stranger and introduce myself." That's okay. Just like everything else in this book, it takes practice. The more you practice, the more confident you will become. Try practicing at a social event, while you are out at night, or in your classes. You may not be great at it right away, but, over time, you will become more comfortable and more effective at walking up to women, introducing yourself, and having a conversation with them.

Great places to use these "meeting people skills" include the campus recreation center, the dining hall, a campus event, computer lab, the library, coffee shop, class, and even at recruitment events! Don't be afraid! If anything, you will just get a chance to practice meeting people. Just remember, the more women you meet, the higher your chances are that more women will likely be involved in the recruitment process, thus giving your chapter and your community better recruitment results.

Conversation Skills

Congratulations! You've learned how to meet people. You are halfway there! So far, you have approached someone that you would normally coast right past, you've used the magic trick to find out her name and a little bit about her, you have figured out what the number one word in her vocabulary is (her name, in case you forgot), and you've used a lead in question to get you started. Awesome.

But, then there's always that totally awkward moment of silence when no one really knows exactly what to say. You can hear a pin drop and you are sure that you look ridiculous. You panic as you try your hardest to think of something, anything, to say that is not going to make you sound like a total dork. Well, from this point on, you can just forget about that uncomfortable feeling, because we are going to teach you the conversation skills you need to master any conversation.

The best way to remain confident in a conversation is to control the conversation. The best way to control the conversation is to minimize your talking and maximize your listening. That's right, *listening.* The best way to monopolize the listening in the conversation is to ask open-ended questions about your conversation partner. The best way to communicate to someone that you care about them is to listen intently to them speak.

Research (and Barbara Streisand) tells us that people need people. In other words, people want to feel like others care about them. Listening is the best way to do that. Another great thing about listening is that you don't have to talk much at all, which means that listening is pretty hard to mess up.

Remember to keep the conversation focused on the other person. What is their favorite word? Their name. And what is their favorite topic? Themselves. Don't even bother talking about the sorority or yourself (unless they ask and, then, only a little). You are trying to learn about them, what they like, what they don't, what they do, where they're from, how they feel, what they value, who they HEART, and so forth. Focus on them, their favorite word, and their favorite topic, and you'll be sure to win every time.

Be sure to pay extra attention to the **Five Fabulous Ways to Master a Conversation** on the next page. The object of these fabulous ways to master conversation is to provide you with open-ended question topics that build rapport, establish common interest or experiences, and focus on them. Remember, stay in control, talk very little about yourself, and always ask questions focused on her.

Five Fabulous Ways to Master Conversation:

FAMILY/FRIENDS

How do you know Ashley? Do you know Lauren? How does your family feel about your decision to attend college away from home?

FAVORITES

I love Tony's Pizza, what do you normally order? Which classes are your favorites? What is your favorite TV show?

FIRSTS

What do you think of your freshman year so far? What are the highlights of your first week of school? What was your first impression of campus? Is this your first time here?

FUN

Where do you hang out on weekends? What do you do outside of classes? Have you seen any good movies lately? What did you do for fun over break?

FROM

Where are you from? How did you end up here? Where do you live now? How often to you go back home? What is your hometown like?

Once you have sparked a conversation with someone, be sure you introduce her to other women. Effective recruiting conversations occur when you use the "Plus One" method. Plus One means that in any conversation, you should have as many members as potential members in the conversation, "Plus One" additional sister. This means if it's a one-on-one conversation, it is more effective to have two sisters and one potential member. If you have two potential members, you need three sisters. You get the picture. We just don't recommend that you get into situations with one potential member in a conversation with ten sisters – that can be a little scary for the potential member and you really don't want to scare them.

You can add a person to your conversation by using a skill called "Bridging." Pretend the person you just met says that she loves to play sand volleyball and you have a sister that is starting a sand volleyball league. You become the bridge between the potential member and your volleyball playing sister using that connection, thus adding her to your conversation. Are you the only sister around? Make sure to connect her with the other sister in a casual setting later on and put these details in the notes section of your Names List for further reference.

NOTE: Some of you have recruitment rules prohibiting "hotboxing," the practice of having more than one sister talking to a potential member at a time. Those rules would, thus, prohibit you from using these skills. It is our suggestion that, regardless of how good our advice may be, you follow your rules. However, we strongly suggest that you and your Panhellenic Community re-evaluate your recruitment rules on a yearly basis to ensure they work for you and your community at that present time. Sometimes, communities have rules in place and they aren't sure why they have them, except for the fact that *"it's always been that way."* Make sure you understand why the rules you have are there. If you can't figure out why they exist, then change them. There is nothing that says that you can't change the rules to work *for* you, instead of against you.

Interaction Skills

Great job! You survived the first few minutes of conversation with a complete stranger. Interaction skills will help you to close your conversation and allow you to continue cultivating the relationship with this new woman, if you so choose.

Since you can't talk forever, you'll eventually have to bring your fabulous conversation to a close. Remember, you control the conversation. Your opening line obviously worked well if you're still talking, so you need an equally good line to close the conversation without losing the relationship with this woman. Remember, if you like her, the idea is to get back together in the near future. Even if you do not COMPLETLEY HEART her, you don't want to totally cut ties with her all together; after all, she has a roommate and friends that you want to meet, too!

Try some of these things:

- "I would love to keep chatting, but I need to get to class. Maybe we can grab lunch together sometime next week?"
- "Thanks for the information; could we talk more later? I can't wait to hear the details."
- "I have a meeting to get to, so let's talk again soon."

WARNING! DO NOT STOP THE CONVERSATION HERE! WARNING! This is certainly not the time to exit! Leaving the conversation without contact information or a time to meet up again leaves you with nothing to show for all of your hard work and fancy magic tricks. It is vital to walk away with an appointment for your next meeting or, at the least, contact information for your new friend. Here are some more "magic tricks" to tactfully do this:

- You: *"Before I get going, here is my contact information. (Write it down on slip of paper in front of her.) Give me a call if you want to get together again. Hey, do you have a number where I can reach you?"*

Voila! You have contact information for another potential member and your Names List just grew by one! You are becoming quite the recruitment Houdini. Don't forget to use her favorite word, her name, to close the conversation. Another great option is to invite her to an upcoming activity. For example:

- You: *"What time are you eating dinner tonight? I'm going to be at the food court with some friends around 6 p.m. You should join us; you've got to eat don't you?"* (It's OK to ask questions you already know the answer to.) *"Great, since I'm going to be on campus around that time anyway, I'll drop by your residence hall around 5:45 and we can go there together. What room number are you in?"* (Note that the question wasn't, *"Do you want me to pick you up?"* The question was, *"What room are you in?"*) *"Here's my phone number in case your plans change. What is the best way I can reach you when I'm on my way?"* (Bingo! You just got her contact info – you go girl!)

Your final magic trick, get your top hat and rabbit ready for this one, it is the best one yet! With this trick, you can double or even triple your productivity with two sentences. Here they are:

- You: *"Do you have a roommate?"* (99% of the time she will, she lives in a residence hall) *"Why don't you go ahead and bring her along with you."*

In the meantime, she says to herself, *"Great, I don't have to meet a group of strangers all alone."* All the while you are thinking, *"Jackpot. Two-for-one special."*

At the conclusion of your event, meal, study group, coffee break, gathering, or whatever you use as the meet-and-greet session for introducing your new friend(s) to your current friends (sisters), you'll need another transition. Don't stress. This one is easy. This is the "keeping in contact" part. You already have her contact information (if you don't, get it NOW), so all you need to do is to invite her to join you and more of your awesome friends for the next gathering.

Always set-up a follow-up meeting, pick her up if possible, and make follow-up phone calls after each meeting. Getting a commitment to another meeting is critical to the success of this system. It may be a little more work than you are used to, but, then again, the results are going to be a lot greater that you're used to as well.

Beyond the First Meeting Skills

After your first meeting together is when it gets REALLY easy. Here is where we could discuss how to be a good friend, but that would make the "skills" section WAY too long. You have probably managed to make at least one or two friends on your own throughout your life, so we'll assume you can do this and will spare you from all the details. From this point on, ALL you have to do is be a friend. Make a friend. Be a friend. Hang out. Do the normal stuff that you already do with your current friends, just add a few new people. Include them like you would include your Little Sis in the sorority without going overboard.

Don't over complicate it. Now is definitely NOT the time for you and your chapter to flip back into formal recruitment mode, break out the crystal punch bowl, the Hawaiian decorations, matching outfits, the chants, and throw a huge recruitment party. Put that stuff away. Lock the door. Lose the key. Just do NORMAL friend stuff. The important thing is that your chapter sets up a consistent system for chapter members to regularly do small activities with prospects. Keep it simple, but systematic.

If you need help thinking of normal activities to do with friends new and old, refer to the activities listed on the next page. Doing these every day activities can take the place of your recruitment events. Do activities, not events. Your chapter will save money and time, plus you'll get to know the potential members a whole lot better. Besides, as a sorority woman, you will look and seem way more normal by doing normal activities instead of doing frilly recruitment events that make you seem like a weirdo to the outside world.

Normal Friend Activities

- TV night

- Breakfast/Coffee/Lunch/Dinner (everybody's got to eat!)

- Shopping

- Watching Sports

- Service/Philanthropy

- Study (now there's a novel idea...)

- Social Events

- Bowling

- Pampering via a pedicure/manicure

- Movies

- Hiking

- Laundry

- Other campus activities (fairs, plays, speakers, musicals, fundraisers, philanthropies)

- Just "hanging out".

*Again, if your rules say that you can't participate in normal, friendly activities with prospective members, today is a great day to start to question those rules.

OK, now you've got the idea. Do normal activities together. That is how real friendships are created. The skills you need to recruit people into your organization are oddly similar to the skills guys use to recruit a date for the weekend (they still do that, right?). They do things like introduce themselves, remember your name, talk about normal stuff, ask for your number, and set up a time to meet again soon in an informal and, possibly, intimate environment. You wouldn't be thrilled if your prospective date immediately asked you, upon your very first meeting, to join him at a barbeque where there will be about 20 other potential girlfriends in attendance, would you?

These activities don't have to take a lot of time or members either. You can have multiple friend activities going on during the same period of time or you can schedule activities for multiple times during the week. It only takes a couple of sisters and a potential member or two. There is little money involved and minimal preparation. All you have to do is make a phone call to one or two of your new friends and have some of your sisters do the same.

At some point, you may develop your relationship enough that you and the chapter members are ready to ask the potential member to join the sorority. This is great news! It can be a long process to build a relationship to the point where you, the chapter, and the potential member would be comfortable asking for a lifetime commitment to/from everyone involved. This is a delicate matter and must be handled with care.

Sealing the Deal Skills

Sealing the deal skills will help you and your chapter members proceed to the next steps in the recruitment process – asking the woman to join. These skills will open your eyes to the possibilities of 100% bid acceptance and much, much more.

Remember what we said in Step Four? You can't recruit who you don't know. This goes vice versa for potential members. They won't join who they don't know. Make sure that the potential members have met plenty of the women in your chapter. This will give them the chance to meet that one specific person who will get them to join. I am sure we all can remember the one person who was the real reason we joined. However, potential members and your chapter will be more sure of the decision if the potential member has met plenty of people in the chapter.

Once they have started meeting more members in the chapter, invite them to chapter events like a service activity or even to the beginning of a chapter meeting (before the business and voting begins). At this point, you're pretty sure you want them to join, but you want the potential member to be just as sure that they want to join. Give them a glimpse into some of the sorority stuff that no one ever talks about – the real day-to-day activities. Also, remember to talk with them about the *benefits* (not features) of membership in your organization.

Once you have done all of that, you are ready to extend a bid.

Stop for Just a Second!

Remember what we told you in the disclaimer.

The following section is important but before you put these lessons into practice you MUST check with your Panhellenic representative or campus professional or both!

We HEART you for following the rules and your campus and National Organization will, too!

Pre-Close Skills

We will provide you with a model to use when asking someone to join your organization, but first let us explain something that will make your ask 100% successful. It's called a "Pre-Close." The Pre-Close is a technique that you can use to guarantee that you will never again offer an invitation for membership to a potential member and have that invitation declined. We know that you're shouting, "TELL ME, TELL ME"! That's right, we are saying that no one will ever say "no" to your chapter's formal bid again. Isn't that how it should be? An invitation to be your sorority sister for life is something that should be handled with utmost care. That's a big, no HUGE, commitment you and the potential member are willing to make. Never again should you invite someone to join your organization if there is a chance they might say no. The Pre-Close shows you how.

The Pre-Close, when prepared for and practiced along with the Quality Responses you developed from Step 5 (remember

Feel*Felt*Found), helps to greatly increase the number of women in your chapter. Here is the magical Pre-Close question: "If we were to ask you to join the sorority right now, would there be any reason you would say no?"

But, wait! Isn't that *bid promising*? Bid promising is a nasty tactic that some chapters still practice. We are vehemently against it, because it has the ability to break hearts and tear up relationships. Do not extend a bid promise. It does not uphold the values of your organization or Panhellenic Community and, besides, it is just tacky. The keys to the Pre-Close are 1) you MUST be absolutely sure, BEYOND A SHADOW OF A DOUBT, that your chapter is going to extend this woman a bid, and 2) you MAY NOT Pre-Close in the formal recruitment process, or at all, if your campus has regulations against it.

Another amazing thing about the Pre-Close is that it allows you to recruit women all year long – even on campuses that have deferred recruitment policies. Your university may not allow you to extend bids to freshmen during certain parts of the year, but that doesn't mean you can't become their friend and find out about their level of interest in sorority life. Recruit year-round, but if your campus has restrictions, save the formal bid for the appropriate time of the year.

The Pre-Close is a technique that you should employ in a separate conversation, prior to extending a bid to a potential new member. Make sure you give the potential member plenty of time to truly come to terms with their concerns.

The Big Ask!

So, now that you have the Pre-Close tucked in your pocket for future use, we will explain how you should ask a potential member to join your organization. It's not as easy as some people think. It's not at all like formal bid matching, where all you do is turn in a list and then eventually get a list back of the people you gave bids to. It is a little more personal than that (as it should be). You are going to be the one that personally extends the bid to someone, face-to-face. That's a big deal. Plus, it is going to take some work and finesse from your side. Below you will find *The Five Stages of a Great Ask* to help you through the process.

Pretty easy stuff, huh? We see you nodding. Well, here are some more tips to make it stellar.

The Five Stages of a Great Ask

1. **Small Talk and Transition:** Start chatting casually; once that begins to subside, move to the next step with a transition.
2. **Ownership Questions:** Pose scenarios within your organization that could include her and ask her what she thinks.
3. **Pre-Close:** Go through your Pre-Close question.
4. **Quality Responses:** Respond to her concerns with your Feel*Felt*Found responses.
5. **Close/Formal Bid:** Ask her to join your organization and the bonds of lifelong sisterhood and friendship.

Helpful Hints to Make Your Ask Successful:

- Do not initially approach her with more than one other member present (remember Plus One).

- Keep the environment comfortable for her on her terms. Do not ask her at the bar, library, or in the sorority house.

- Dress appropriately. If you want to be taken seriously, dress the part.

- Practice what you are going to say. Know how to answer common questions and objections by reviewing your Quality Responses and reminding yourself what you like about her. Try role-playing with other sisters for additional practice.

- Be Real! This is not a cold call or a sales meeting. You're about to ask one of your best friends to join your family of sisters.

- Compliment her on the qualities of her character that make her stand out as a woman.

- Keep the conversation about her.

- Remember Feel*Felt*Found. Her commitment is just on the other side of her concerns. Help her get over those concerns using Quality Responses.

What an Ask Might Look Like:

Small Talk:

- This is simple -- anytime you ask someone to join your organization, start off with normal, friendly small talk.

(For reference, review the previous section, "5 Fabulous Ways to Master Conversation.")

Transition statement:

- *"We could probably talk about _____ all day, but there is something else I really want to talk with you about."*

Ownership questions:

- *"Our sorority has been through a lot this year.* ***If you were leading a group like ours, what do you think you would do?"***

- *"You are one of the greatest women I have ever known. I think it would be an honor for me to call you my sorority sister someday.* ***What do you think?"***

- *"I think you're a strong individual with a lot of potential. A true leader with character and the passion for helping others. I want you to know that I've got a lot of respect for you. Those are the same qualities our sorority looks for in its members.* ***What do you think it would take for us to attract more women like yourself?"***

- *"You know the sorority is one of the most important parts of my life, right? I've talked with the sisters and they think you're the type of person that we need as we move forward to the next level.* ***What do you think?"***

Pre-close:

- *"Sally, if the sorority extended you a bid for membership, what would you say?"*

Quality Responses

- *"I know how you **feel**. I **felt** the same way. Let me share with you what I **found**..."*
- *"Did I completely answer that question for you? Do you still feel like that concern would prohibit you from joining the group? Considering that, is there any other concern that would prevent you from saying yes?"*

Close/Formal Bid:

- *"Sally, this is a big night. The main reason I came over to see you is because I'm representing my entire sorority as I ask you an important question. We would like to formally extend to you a bid for membership to our sorority. Will you accept our invitation?"*

Great Job! The *Ask* is the most important part of the entire step. After all, how many women were missed because no one ever asked them to join?

Public Relations Skills

You are probably thinking, what is Public Relations doing here? In fact, why is it even in this book? You have also probably noticed that Step 6 focuses on interpersonal relationship building and not mass marketing or building relationships with the public.

The Eight Steps to Limitless Possibility focus on the power of personal relationships, encouraging a shift away from depending on the frills, the glitz, and the glam of *Static Recruitment*. These things merely mask the true purpose of sorority and sorority recruitment. We highly encourage a shift from fancy desserts, decorations, matching t-shirts, chanting, and all the other things that push the focus away from what you are trying accomplish. After all, how many of your members actually joined your organization because you had cool matching outfits or because they liked your chant? We would wager to say none. These frills intimidate women out of the process more than anything else. While these things can be very valuable in developing a great image for your organization, they shouldn't be relied upon for growing and developing your membership, especially during recruitment.

Can you imagine the producer of *Saturday Night Live* recruiting new actresses by passing out t-shirts with a catchy phrase or by offering the BEST cheesecake in town to hundreds of women who really aren't funny OR good at acting? If you want to have a top-level organization, do what other top-level organizations do – build personal relationships with people who have common values centered around the true organizational purpose.

PR Questions to Consider

- If you were to create a t-shirt that expressed everything that you stand for, what would it say?

- How many of your sisters joined because they knew someone in your chapter? Because they were a legacy? Because they made a connection with another sister?

- How many women came to your organization for the first time because of formal recruitment? How many of those women stayed because of the people they connected with? If they had made no connection, would they have stayed for the cool events and yummy desserts? Would they have stayed for life?

- How many members in your chapter right now joined because of printed materials that they saw? Is that why you joined?

- What do the events that you hold during recruitment or to attract new members say about you? What do they say about your chapter? Your community? Your sisters nationwide?

- What three words best represent everything that your organization stands for? How else could you use those on promotional materials? (Think outside the t-shirt box!)

- What makes your chapter or Greek Community actually UNIQUE?

- Why does your chapter exist, if there are a dozen others just like it on your campus?

GO FOR IT, GIRL!

Experience the limitless possibilities that await your chapter right away by applying the ideas provided here:

- ♥ Practice your Meeting People Skills at your next social function. The skills you need to recruit a new sister or get another name for your list are the same skills you use to meet that cute guy you've been eyeing all night.

- ♥ Use your Conversation Skills during interactions with people in your classes. Even try role-playing with your sisters using the Five Fabulous Ways to Master a Conversation for practice.

- ♥ Incorporate the skills in Step 6 into your new member education plan. The sooner your members learn this information and start practicing, the better. Practice makes permanent.

- ♥ Identify some Normal Friend Activities that you and your members can do every week together in small groups and, then, start inviting people from your Names List to come as well. You can have multiple activities going on at the same time.

- ♥ Rethink your frills. Cut your recruitment budget in half and try to work with that amount by paring down the glitz and glam of your recruitment events. Invest some of that money into a charity, educational programming, or by investing in more of *our* books or training services ☺.

HOW LONG?

At this point you might be thinking, this is all great, but how in the world am I going to accomplish this? Where do I begin? How do I keep it going? And how in the world do I get the rest of my chapter involved?

Well, first of all, take a deep breath, then slowly let it out, and repeat. Don't worry, we weren't going to abandon you with all of this information without teaching you how to use it and put it into practice! The How Long? section of the book is just the stuff you need!

Steps 7 and 8 will help you to continue to build upon all the other steps in the book. These last two steps may be the shortest and the simplest; however, they might also be the most important. DO NOT SKIP THIS SECTION. See, we knew you were thinking about it. Don't try to deny it. It's the EIGHT steps to limitless possibility, not SIX. So, keep reading!

"Aerodynamically the bumblebee shouldn't be able to fly, but the bumblebee doesn't know that so it goes on flying anyway."

~Mary Kay Ash~

STEP 7: GROW WISER

Step 7 is the pursuit of wisdom. It is by far the most important and influential of the Eight Steps. This step requires the most persistence, but will help you achieve the greatest returns. Aren't you glad you kept reading?

Wisdom, as a value, is at the heart of sorority life. All sororities, like your own, encourage their members to pursue knowledge and education for the greater good of women everywhere. Wisdom is a value that we share as Panhellenic women and it is the heart of Step 7. But, what does wisdom or the greater pursuit of intelligence really have to do with sorority recruitment? Great question. We'll explain.

So, there is this sorority that has existed for more than 100 years. Their founders were intelligent women who were the epitome of what a great woman should be. It was 103 years ago that this sorority was founded, and it was about 103 years ago that this sorority created its now established traditions, habits, and recruitment practices. Since their creation, the sorority has done little to improve, grow, or alter their behaviors, including their recruitment practices. Nonetheless, the sorority has existed fairly well for the past 103 years. They have built chapters all over the country and have maintained a proud tradition of excellence.

Overall, this sorority is a great organization. Somewhere along the line, however, the sorority reached a membership plateau. For some reason, the sorority was no longer experiencing success in recruitment. Their membership wasn't growing. The sorority remained on this plateau for many years, decades even. Since this time, the sorority has maintained a constant state of good – not great – just good. Is there something that this sorority is doing wrong? More importantly, are there things they could be doing better? What are they missing?

The single answer to all of these questions is wisdom. This sorority, which has, over time, seen some success, has never looked beyond their own traditions, habits, and recruitment practices for ways to improve. They didn't commit to constantly seeking new wisdom as an organization. They never looked to a book on sorority recruitment (probably because there wasn't one until now). They never asked for or brought in assistance from outside the sorority. They assumed that the founders knew best and they would just keep maintaining the very same systems that their founders put in place. This group is lacking wisdom.

Growing wiser increases your overall awareness: an awareness of opportunities to grow and learn, an awareness of new practices and methods, an awareness of where to go for help, and overall an awareness of what works and what does not. Awareness is something that this sorority is clearly lacking.

To have your recruitment efforts produce greater results, you and your chapter need to continually grow wiser and continually seek a greater awareness. In life, we make mistakes, find what works, find what doesn't, and then learn from those mistakes. These life lessons are likewise applicable in recruitment. In recruitment, there are mistakes, there are things that work, and there are things that do not. We learn from these personal experiences, adjust, and move on, growing wiser along the way.

"Lessons learned through personal experiences" is just a sugar-coated way of saying "failure." That's right, we said it, that awful, horrible word – failure. But, here is a little known secret: Failure is not bad. Failure is good. That's right, we are promoting failure! Go ahead girl, FAIL!

You and your chapter should learn to see your failures as stepping stones in growing wiser. Eventually, these stepping stones will lead to your ultimate success. The more you fail, the more you succeed. We know, it sounds crazy, but trust us. The more you fail, the more you learn, thus the more you eventually will succeed. Knowledge is power.

What recruitment practices have you tried and failed? What recruitment practices has your chapter tried that only got mediocre results? What did you learn from these experiences? How did you improve it for the future? Isn't this whole process helping you to grow wiser?

Besides being smarter, having a greater awareness, and learning from the failure of your own experiences, you can also learn from the experiences of others. By seeking wisdom from the experiences of others, you can minimize the mistakes your chapter has to make (history always repeats itself if you don't learn from it). The key to this is to seek the advice of the right people. An intelligent woman would never ask an accountant to perform surgery, nor would she ask a doctor to do her taxes. Likewise, she does not ask her unqualified friends, family, or alumnae members for advice on effective recruitment practices. She asks the experts.

As you look to create an atmosphere of limitless possibilities within your organization, remember that the people who tell you that something is impossible are the people who gave up too soon, not the experts. The experts are who you go to for qualified advice on recruitment. Here are three ways to do that:

Mentorship

The advice of a professional is priceless in saving time, money, and energy. Ask those who know about the things you need to know. Find a personal "fan club" of qualified experts invested in your personal and chapter's success. Find other chapters on your campus or within your international sorority who are committed to limitless possibilities and mentor each other. Ask a successful college or sorority alumnus, parent, professor, or administrator to serve as a "success advisor." Ask someone who recruits or who does sales for a living to help your chapter re-shape their recruitment and "sales" practices. Make your mentoring a part of your daily life.

Reading

There is no replacement for knowledge gained through reading. That's why all of your teachers and professors since preschool have made you do it! As it turns out, there are a lot of books on the market that can help sororities with recruitment, they just don't say

"RECRUITMENT" or "RECRUITMENT FOR DUMMIES" in big bold letters on the front. We recommend reading for at least 20 minutes a day (each and every day, even if you have to force yourself) from the list of Recommended Recruitment Resources on the following pages. There is nothing more powerful than knowing that 300 or fewer pages can bestow the life's work and knowledge of some of the world's most powerful men and women upon you. What business and world leaders can you read about to learn tips on growing and sustaining a strong organization?

Outside Learning

Attending conferences, workshops, seminars, speaker series, and continuing/outside educational programs can be one of the best ways to grow wiser. What it comes down to is exposing yourself and your organization to as many people, ideas, and opportunities as you can. Search for opportunities that allow you to see how other sororities/fraternities, organizations, or businesses grow and become successful. Then, try to adapt those ideas for your organization's use. Attend your sorority's regional and inter/national events. Go to the non-mandatory lectures on campus. Find out what other student organizations are doing on your campus or other campuses for leadership development and recruitment. Ask your student life professionals (your Greek advisor, Dean of Students, etc.) for their recommendations!

Becoming a chapter and sorority community with the necessary wisdom to be successful in recruitment takes a commitment to seek out knowledge from beyond your normal circles and to consider how that knowledge applies to your needs. Growing wiser is so much more than just reading or finding a mentor. It's about awareness, learning from your failures, and continuously finding new ways to expand your knowledge. The wisdom you gain from doing these things will immediately begin to transform your chapter. Just remember, it is equally as important to teach as it is to utilize your learned knowledge.

We have become knowledgeable and successful recruitment experts (and authors of a book on recruitment) due mostly to the fact that we read the words of people smarter than us as often as possible. Remember, we used to be really bad at recruitment too, but then we learned through our own experiences and failures, plus the experiences and failures of others, that there were amazing recruitment possibilities sitting right beneath our noses – we just needed to be willing to seek out the wisdom necessary to achieve the results.

In case you don't believe us on this "growing wiser" stuff, here are some thoughts on wisdom from some other experts:

"Each of us has that right, that possibility, to invent ourselves daily. If a person does not invent herself, she will be invented. So, to be bodacious enough to invent ourselves is wise."

Maya Angelou

"My philosophy is that not only are you responsible for your life, but doing the best at this moment puts you in the best place for the next moment."

Oprah Winfrey

"You'll be the same person in five years as you are today with two exceptions: the people you associate with, and the books that you read."

Charlie "Tremendous" Jones

"I only want people around me who can do the impossible."

Elizabeth Arden

"How many cares one loses when one decides not to be something but to be someone."

Coco Chanel

"You gain strength, courage, and confidence by every experience in which you really stop to look fear in the face…You must do the thing you think you cannot do."

Eleanor Roosevelt

Recommended Recruitment Resources

Good Guys: The Eight Steps to Limitless Possibility for Fraternity Recruitment
Matt Mattson & Josh Orendi

The Leadership Institute – Women with Purpose, Inc.
www.theleadershipinstitute-wwp.org

You're in Charge - Now What?
Thomas Neff & James Citrin

How to Talk to Anyone
Leil Lowndes

The Power of Nice
Linda Thaler & Robin Koval

Women Make the Best Salesmen
Marion Luna Brem

Campus CEO
Randal Pinkett

Nice Girls Don't Get the Corner Office
Lois Frankel

How to Say It for Women
Phyllis Mindell

Never Eat Alone
Keith Ferrazzi

How to Win Friends and Influence People
Dale Carnegie

7 Habits of Highly Effective People
Stephen Covey

The Magic of Thinking Big
David Schwartz

Good to Great
Jim Collins

The Fine Art of Small Talk
Debra Fine

The Tipping Point
Malcolm Gladwell

21 Irrefutable Laws of Leadership
Maxwell & Ziglar

Think and Grow Rich
Napoleon Hill

Purple Cow
Seth Godin

The Networking Survival Guide
Diane Darling

100 Ways to Motivate Yourself
100 Ways to Motivate Others
Steve Chandler

20 Something- 20 Everything

Christine Hassler

Alpha Girls: Understanding the New American Girl and How She is
Changing the World
Dan Kindlon

GO FOR IT GIRL!

Experience the limitless possibilities that await your chapter right away by applying the ideas provided here:

♥ Give the list of Recommended Recruitment Resources to your friends and family for holiday gift ideas. Better yet, use the library on campus.

♥ Commit at least 20 minutes each and every day to reading from the Resources for Further Development list.

♥ Ask you student life and headquarters professionals about any upcoming conferences, workshops, or seminars that could help to improve your chapter

♥ Make two lists. On one list, write down everything on which you think your chapter could use some advice. On the other list, write down every person that you know who is either smarter than you or has more experience than you. Finish the list by writing down two or three famous people that you admire and would like to meet. Try to match the needs on the first list to the wisdom on the second list and, for those that have matches, ask for mentorship. Yes, even ask the famous people! For those without matches, we suggest you just keep looking for more smart people to meet.

♥ Have a "failure meeting" with your chapter's key leaders and a select group of alumnae from various years. Talk about all the successes and failures the chapter has had over the years, then ask what you can learn from them now.

"Perseverance is failing nineteen times and succeeding the twentieth."

~ Julie Andrews~

STEP 8: REPEAT

Wash. Rinse. Repeat. Good advice. Sometimes you need to do things more than once for them to be truly effective. Imagine if you only washed you hair once, say about 15 years ago, and never did it again. Shampoo only works because you keep using it over and over again as part of a daily routine (for some of you, it may be an every-other-day routine or whatever, but you get the general idea). The same goes for The Eight Steps. They are only effective if you take them beyond the pages of this book and put them into practice daily – not for a week, a month, or a semester, but repeatedly over time and for generations to come. The Eight Steps will only create *Dynamic Recruitment* success in your chapter or in your community if you build the steps into your sorority culture. Building the *Dynamic Recruitment* system into the culture of your chapter begins with you, spans out to your membership, and continues with repeated support, education, and reinforcement.

Step 8 is a point of transition and transformation; it is now time for you to transform from student to teacher. You should share this information with as many people possible and as soon as possible. You must talk about the lessons you've learned in this book in order for the system to take shape within your chapter or Panhellenic community. Your responsibility is to now pass this information along to the rest of your members and Greek community, so that they may begin practicing *Dynamic Recruitment* daily – repeating it daily.

This eight step process is designed to improve the *quality* and *quantity* of your chapter membership to the degree of your choosing. When the lessons, practices, and ideas of The Eight Steps are practiced (and repeated) daily, you will begin to see a revolutionary transformation in your chapter – but it takes repetition for it to stick. The work you are doing will suddenly seem like second nature the more you practice it and just go for it, sort of like learning to tie your shoes, brushing your teeth, driving a car, or shampooing your hair.

How is this possible? Well, you've managed to create a change in your habits or *patterns of behavior*. Remember in the S.P.A.M. section when we talked about patterns of behavior? Those things, like tying your shoes or driving a car, that once took your full concentration, are second nature. You might even be able to do them with you eyes closed (though, we really hope you aren't trying to drive your car with your eyes closed!) When you first learned to tie your shoes or drive a car it took a lot of concentration. A few months later, the intricate steps involved in driving a car became an unconscious pattern of behavior or like second nature to you. The steps of this book can become second nature, too, with a little concentrated effort and repetition, just like learning to tie your shoes or drive! You didn't try driving just one time, then walking everywhere for the next three months, only to try driving again and expect to be great at it, did you?

Step 8 is very simple. The key to making the whole Eight Step *Dynamic Recruitment* model work is simply repetition.

The Plan

There is an old saying we know everyone has heard, "Practice makes perfect." However, what we believe it should really say is "Practice makes permanent." The education process for your members should begin immediately upon their entrance into the organization and be continued during their undergraduate experience. By the time your members graduate, they will be "experts" and should be teaching other new members all this wisdom. However, before you start repeating things, you need to understand exactly what it is you are repeating. You need a plan. Your plan is the strategy you chapter is going to use as a means to implement The Eight Steps to Dynamic Recruitment.

How do you "plan" to use the Eight Steps?

A great and effective plan means that attracting the best women on your campus will take much more than matching outfits, loud cheering, and delectable cheesecake (cheesecake seems the preferred dessert for preference night from our experiences). That's right, we said it, put the matching outfits back in the drawer, save your voices, and don't bother with the cheesecake.

Instead, consider treating your chapter like Vogue Magazine. It is highly unlikely that the Human Resources Department of Vogue would search for a new editor-and-chief by placing an ad in USA Today which included pictures of the women who work at Vogue (all in matching outfits), posed cheek to cheek, with the offer of having the best cafeteria (plus the best cheesecake) as a reason someone would want the job. As ridiculous as this sounds (and all this talk of cheesecake is making us hungry), many campuses have seen these same or similarly embarrassing attempts by sororities to attract the best leaders on campus Ask yourself, did you join because your sorority had the best cheesecake, outfits, house, or cutest girls? We didn't think so.

Mary Kay Cosmetics is probably a better example for us to use. This company started small (just like every sorority did), but grew to become one of the most widely recognized cosmetic corporations among women internationally. Though their vision has always been top notch, anyone will tell you that Mary Kay's true success lies within their business plan. Mary Kay offers women the opportunity to grow within their own realm and limits. It gives women the chance to have financial independence and career advancement. Their business plan was simple, repeatable, and offered anyone the opportunity to be involved and succeed (as long as they followed the plan repeatedly).

Today, Mary Kay is seen and available everywhere, due in part to the successful business plan as well as the dedicated consultants who carried it out repeatedly over time.

Every great business or organization has the same ingredients – the right people executing the right plan. Sororities are no different. You need a great team of sisters to create a great plan and to start the process off right.

The Eight Steps to Limitless Possibility provide you with a framework for making your chapter's plan for recruitment and long-term success. This is a system that can make, not break, your chapter and some of the most influential, successful, and exciting young women on your campus. The more people that get on board, the better - eventually, the system will do the same thing for your entire Panhellenic community.

Roundtable

So, now you know that in order to effectively implement The Eight Steps into your chapter, you must have a plan. Chances are, as one of the few enlightened leaders of your chapter, you are going to need some help coming up with that plan and then even more help implementing it. Most sororities get too caught up in leadership positions, titles, policies, and committees – especially when it comes to recruitment. Sororities are so used to putting all of the responsibility on the Recruitment Chair or Recruitment Team that they don't know any other way to get things done. We suggest creating our version of a Roundtable to solve these problems.

A Roundtable is simple. It is basically a meeting of the minds, any minds. You just need to get a group of people together who enjoy recruitment or who want to be involved in the creation and implementation of your new, improved chapter "plan." It can start with as few as three people. Get together weekly for a meeting to discuss the ideas in the book and start your own revolution. You don't need the whole chapter on board to get started. Margaret Mead said it best when she said, "Never doubt that a small group of thoughtful committed citizens can change the world. Indeed, it's the only thing that ever has."

We know that Pareto's Principle holds true in most organizations and also holds true in this situation – 20% of the people produce 80% of the results. We also learned in Step Four the important difference between Wes (the ass) and Joey (the stallion). Remember, do not invest your time in the mules that do not want to be a part of the process (some of them may even complain about it). Capitalize on the stallions when you are putting together your Roundtable, as they are the 20% that are willing to put in the most effort to get your ideas off the ground and make the plan work. Now, you may already be a rock star organization and have more than 20% of your members who are ready to rock and roll. If so, awesome! You are way ahead of the game. If not, they better get moving because greatness doesn't wait around for mediocrity!

Purpose of a Roundtable

- Begin to formulate your chapter plan on how to implement the Eight Steps of Dynamic Recruitment.

- Serve as mentors to the general membership with ongoing support for both the chapter's plan and the Eight Step model.

- Constantly support, promote, and teach the Eight Steps to all members.

- Hold all members accountable for the Eight Steps, putting names ON the list, taking names OFF the list, carrying out the chapter PLAN, and continuing to GROW WISER!

- Most importantly, continue to build the organization's DREAM!

Roundtable Meeting Agenda

We've put together some questions to use during your first (of many) Roundtable meetings.

1. How much time are we spending on the basics (people and purpose)? How can we improve that amount of time?

2. How have you lived our organization's values this week? (A.C.E. your values.)

3. What did you do this week to feed your WILD DREAM?

4. Where will you meet five (5 for 5) new women tomorrow?

5. How has this organization enhanced your life this week?

6. What have you read lately that could help the organization?

7. How can we make our chapter's plan better?

8. How can we better educate the chapter on the plan?

9. When and where are we meeting next?

GO FOR IT, GIRL!

Experience the limitless possibilities that await your chapter right away by applying the ideas provided here:

♥ Organize your Roundtable. If you notice a few sisters who also seem interested in a recruitment revolution, ask them to read this book and then join your Roundtable each week.

♥ Start formulating your chapter's plan. You can't put the Eight Steps into practice for your chapter until you figure out how you are going to do it. Use the "Go For It, Girl" sections of the book to help you build your plan.

♥ Use the Eight Steps to guide your new member education program. Start their education from the very beginning and continue to "wash, rinse, and repeat" over the course of membership.

♥ Let this book work for you. Ask two of your sisters to read it (maybe even an advisor). Watch as the excitement in the chapter grows!

WHO DOES ALL THIS?

You may be saying to yourself, "All this information is really nice and seems like a good idea, but isn't this all supposed to be the job of the Recruitment Chair? Isn't all of this just making the Recruitment Chair's job harder? Are these ladies out of their minds?"

Fair questions. To put it plainly, however, the answers are no, no, and not always. This Eight Step system is not just for the Recruitment Chair of your chapter. Furthermore, this eight step system actually makes the job of Recruitment Chair easier.

The only way to make this system really work is to have a small group of chapter members committed to changing your current system. The Recruitment Chair can then become the "manager" of the process. It should NOT be the Recruitment Chair's job to meet everyone you are putting on the Names List. Your results won't be that great if you take that approach with this new process. The Recruitment Chair should, however, take the lead in managing all of the members of the chapter (or, at the least, the Roundtable sessions) and ensuring that they are performing their simple, daily habits that will lead to your chapter's success.

Your Recruitment Chair can guide your members through all of the activities in this book. It should be the Recruitment Chair's job to ensure that the right recruitment efforts are at the top of the chapter's priority list.

This book outlines patterns of behavior that each member of your chapter can adopt. If you want to achieve greater results, you must do greater things than you're currently doing. Challenge your chapter to redefine the role of Recruitment Chair and to redefine the role each sister plays in the year round recruitment process.

THE EIGHT STEPS IN REVIEW

The Eight Steps to Limitless Possibility provides a framework for your sorority's recruitment revolution. Follow the tips listed in this book, ask yourself the tough questions, and make The Eight Steps your chapter's new and improved system of operation.

Step 1 reminds you to focus your energy on the two basic fundamentals of your organization: People and Purpose. Do things that attract a lot of high quality sisters and make sure everyone is dedicated to your chapter's purpose.

Step 2 promotes Achieving, Communicating, and Expecting your organization's values in everything that you do as an organization. If you skip Step 2, you're just another club causing trouble for the rest of us.

Step 3 pushes you to build your chapter's dream. Get your sisters to build a recruitment dream that is so big that they will do whatever it takes – everyday – to make it into a reality. The motivation to do the small things right is based on building a big enough dream. Remember, focus on the stallions in your group, not the mules.

Step 4 stretches your understanding of your potential audience and helps you understand where you can find the thousands of future sisters that are sitting out there waiting to be asked.

Step 5 implores you to know your product before you go out and try to sell it. Understand and be able to communicate the value and benefits of your organization, so that when the opportunity arises, you can sell anyone on how great it is to be in your sorority.

Step 6 builds your interpersonal skills so that you can be confident going out into the world, shaking hands, developing friendships, and recruiting sisters.

Step 7 teaches you that to improve; you must be willing to learn the lessons that make you wiser. Recruitment results will stay the same unless you continually seek out new ideas, new strategies, and new systems to take your chapter from mediocre performance to amazing results.

Step 8 instructs you to repeatedly do the little things to unearth big results. Build a new system for your chapter in which each member is taught and re-taught each component of The Eight Steps.

This system ensures success, not just for this semester, but for years and years to come. Each step is necessary. They depend upon one another. Do them all and watch your results grow exponentially.

FREQUENTLY ASKED QUESTIONS

We've noticed that the people who talk with us about The Eight Steps to Limitless Possibility have certain questions that come up over and over again. Here are the most common questions we've been asked, along with some quick answers. We hope these will help as you start to share these ideas with others in your chapter or on your campus.

Question: Where do I start?

Answer: What can you do in the next 24 hours that will make a difference? The process starts with baby steps. Start with small changes and the big ones will follow. We recommend beginning by dream building, assembling your roundtable, teaching others this recruitment system, and creating your Names List.

Question: What if I don't want a big chapter?

Answer: *Quantity* drives *quality*. It doesn't matter if you want to grow 40 times larger or stay the same size. Your chapter benefits from simply having more women from which to choose.

Question: How can I ever get my women to do any of this?

Answer: Leave the door open for all, but get started with just a few. What impact could your top five women have if they each recruited five women like themselves? The Roundtable concept works great for a practical answer to this question.

Question: What if our chapter needs to work on internal issues first?

Answer: Remember the basics: People and Purpose. Save managing your mules for later. New leaders and new members will solve almost all of your problems. The answer to most sorority problems really is recruitment.

Question: I know all this already. What's the point?

Answer: To know and not do is to not know.

Question: Where do I go for more information?

Answer: http://www.PhiredUp.com/

Throughout this book, we have provided suggestions for putting The Eight Steps to Limitless Possibility into action. Now is the time to go for it. The change that is possible may not be incredibly easy, but it really is as simple as GOING FOR IT, GIRL. We've merely provided a system that achieves results as long as you are committed to working the system. The choice is truly yours.

Think of it this way -- most personal fitness trainers suggest that the hardest part of any exercise program is just getting started! The same is true of this program. It takes several days or even weeks to see significant results from working out in the gym. And, even with small rewards and improvements along the way, it takes approximately 21 days for the gym to become a pattern of behavior or habit. Similarly, the hardest part of this program is just getting started and making it through the first stages of developing a pattern of behavior. The key is to build momentum, one day and one step at a time, and soon the body will feel deprived by NOT going to the gym or, in this case, you'll feel robbed by not doing the things that will make your sorority great.

The Eight Step Process is Simple:

1. Understand what your sorority is and how it works.

2. Commit to your purpose, then A.C.E. it.

3. Dream of what you could be, then let that motivate you, your chapter members, and your potential members.

4. Identify your organization's potential: Who do you want and who is available?

5. Know what you're offering and know how to communicate it.

6. Do the little things to get who and what you want.

7. Continually grow wiser.

8. Repeat the process over and over.

Phew! You made it to the end and we're so proud of you! Thanks for sticking with us, gals. We believe in you, just like you SHOULD believe in your chapter. And, if you need us, we are here to help you. Feel free to contact us:

Jessica Gendron: Jessica@phiredup.com
Colleen Coffey: Colleen@phiredup.com

www.PhiredUp.com

You can do this!

Go for it, girl – *Change your HE♥RT and fall in LOVE with Recruitment!*

ABOUT THE AUTHORS

Colleen Coffey brings the Phired Up team a dynamic perspective on recruitment and organizational culture. As a Performance Consultant for Phired Up, she is a charming presenter, a thorough consultant with the professional experience and passion for working with college students, and an extensive knowledge base in the area of sorority recruitment. Colleen achieved a Bachelor of Social Work from Belmont University and graduated from Eastern Illinois University with a Master's Degree in College Student Affairs after having completed her thesis research, a program evaluation on sorority recruitment. Colleen works full time as the Program Manager for The Leadership Institute - Women with Purpose, Inc. and is a speaker for "The Heard," The National Mental Health Awareness Campaign's speaker's bureau.

Jessica Gendron brings to the Phired Up team a wealth of experience and skill when it comes to organizational recruitment and fraternity/sorority culture. As a performance consultant for Phired Up, she is a charismatic and energetic presenter, as well as a skilled consultant. Jessica has professional experience working with college students, which includes an extensive knowledge base in sorority recruitment, values-based initiatives, risk management and community development. Jessica has a Bachelor of Art in Graphic Design from Eastern Illinois University and a Master of Science in Higher Education and Student Affairs from Indiana University - Bloomington. Jessica is currently a Greek advisor at Washington University in Saint Louis as well as a national volunteer for Alpha Sigma Tau sorority.

MY NEW RECRUITMENT PLAN

_____

_____

_____

_____

_____

_____

_____

_____

_____

_____

_____

_____

_____

_____

_____

_____

_____

_____

_____

_____